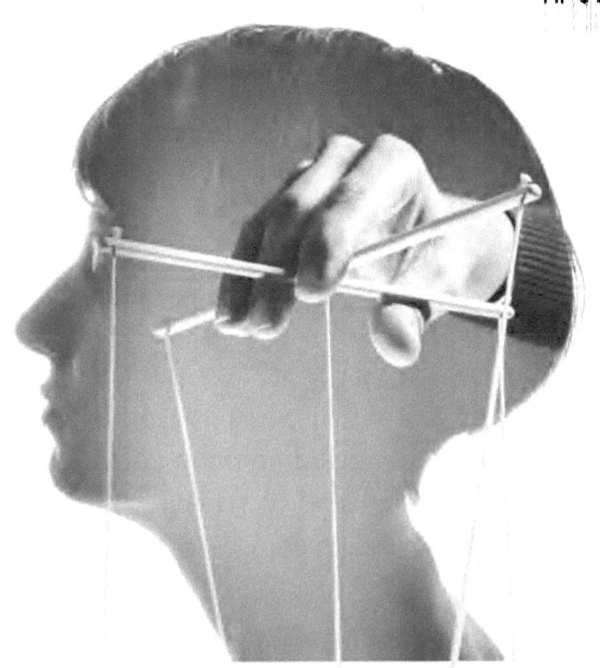

BREAKING STRINGS

Pinocchio Tells The Truth About Being Free

Patricia Pillard McCulley

Published by
Interdimensional Press
Brentwood, CA

Copyright © 2020 by Patricia Pillard McCulley

All rights reserved. No part of this publication may be reproduced or transmitted in any form or by any means, electronic or mechanical, including photocopy, recording, or any information storage and retrieval system, without permission in writing from the copyright owner.

ISBN
978-0-9911970-9-5

Library of Congress Control Number
2020947618

Printed in the United States of America

Dedication

This book is dedicated to my grandchildren, Daphne Lois Saurman and Ryan Jeffrey Saurman. I have written *Breaking Strings* with the desire of sharing my thoughts with you about life, love, inner peace, and happiness, in essence, becoming free.

This is also dedicated to all young people coming of age in our crazy world. As I write this dedication, our world is still being held captive by the COVID-19 virus pandemic. We are faced with racial and political divisions that need to be healed. And, too, our planet, people, and animals are in distress in the West with the wildfires, and in the East with tornadoes, and hurricanes.

My hope is that this book will help all of you gain insight into what it means to be free so you can handle your life challenges with understanding and resolution, leading to inspiration, gratefulness and compassion for all.

My Note to You

The idea for this book came after a friend read my first book, *Finding the Lost UNIVERSAL PRINCIPLES: The Three Little Pigs unlock the door*. He said he had teenagers and they really needed to know "this stuff." *Breaking Strings* includes the universal principles, but much more — the information I wish I'd had as a young person.

I've dedicated *Breaking Strings* to all young people coming of age in our crazy world today. COVID-19 is still raging. Many of you have lost loved ones and are grieving. Many are suffering from the shutdown of our economy. Many have lost their businesses. Many are enduring hardships because of loss of income from their jobs. I believe there will be a vaccine available eventually and the virus will no longer spread, but the effects remain. In addition there are wildfires in the West and hurricanes in the East causing major disruptions to many others. My heart goes out to all of you.

We have an option as to how we want to respond to our own situation. We can be angry, and bitter, and depressed or we can rise above those negative feelings to help others in some way — be it a smile, a kind word, a card in the mail, a small gift, or a monetary donation to a cause. We may see the good that is developing. We will not go back to "normal." Being born are new ways of communication, transportation, entertainment, even the way we treat others.

The United States is very divided as this book goes to press. Many factions are sparring against each other that can end if we discover we are stronger when we work together and truly act like a group of united states as our forefathers envisioned.

Perhaps by the time you read *Breaking Strings* the craziness will have begun to lessen. This is not just a job for "them," it's for each one of us, in our own way, to come together and heal. As young people, we elders look to you to stand on our shoulders and help us mend, with your thoughts of inclusiveness and love for the planet. You are the ones we've been waiting for.

Breaking Strings is not meant to be the final word on freedom and life, for the moment this book is published, it will be in the past, and new ideas will be forming. You may want to add another chapter of your own to this book or add another to the Universal Principles list.

May you always be a seeker and one filled with curiosity, for to be truly alive you will always be learning.

Patricia McCulley
November 2020

WHERE IT'S AT

Dedication /iii

My Note to You / iv

Read This First / 1

Chapter 1: Freedom Is An Inside Job/ 7

Chapter 2: Truths and Misconceptions / 13

Chapter 3: Lessons From A Wooden Boy / 23

Chapter 4: An Inkling And A Nagging From A Cricket / 29

Chapter 5: Is School A Problem For You? By SJ Farry / 33

Chapter 6: Sex And Sexuality / 39

Chapter 7: Decisions, Decisions, Decisions / 47

Chapter 8: To Trust Or Not To Trust / 61
        What you can't count on /64
        What you can count on / 66

Chapter 9: The "How To Be Happy And Peaceful" Test / 71

Chapter 10: *The Universal Principles Book for Life* / 75

    #1: All Is One / 76
        Physical / 77
        People / 79
        Religion / 82
        Time And Space / 92

#2: The Balance of Life / 97

#3: The Unseen Controls The Seen / 103

#4: Cause and Effect Always Occur Together / 118

#5: Change Is A Constant / 122

#6: We Are Spiritual Beings / 125

#7: It's All About Energy and Vibration / 130

Chapter 11: The Definition Of Success / 137

Final Thoughts:
    You're The One We've Been Waiting For / 143

Acknowledgments / 147

Appendix A: A Whale in Jail / 151

Appendix B: Advice from Bill Gates / 153

Appendix C: Rules for Being Human by Ann Landers / 155

Appendix D: The Four Agreements / 157

Appendix E: A Message from Gautama Buddha / 159

"Who Looks outside, Dreams;
Who Looks Inside, Awakens."

Dr. Carl Gustaf Jung, M.D.
Psychiatrist and Psychologist

"Your relationship with yourself sets the tone for
every other relationship you have."

Dr. Robert Holden, Ph.D
Psychologist

READ THIS FIRST

Congratulations on your interest in *Breaking Strings*. Reading this book is the beginning of your taking control of your life, for in-depth answers to your questions, for spending time on things that truly matter.

Your parents and grandparents had some of these same questions when they were your age, but their answers might not fit anymore. You are part of a new generation that likely needs different answers.

If you picked up this book because you feel overwhelmingly depressed or feel your life is worthless or feel you may be in danger from another person, please reach out for help.

Right now.

Help can come in many different ways: a hotline, a trusted adult like a parent, a guardian, a teacher, or in the form of a professional counselor. Even if you don't like to do therapy or it seems too embarrassing, you need to try to overcome those feelings and learn to express yourself. Adults who are truly smart ask for help when they need it. Your future self will thank you for deciding to be open to guidance.

You Matter! www.movingyourmind.com is a site worth checking out. They have articles and resources for teens and young adults. They state:

You are not alone in your anxiety and depression. Being a teenager is an emotional time filled with many unknowns and an incredible amount of social, academic and personal pressures and problems. Moving your Mind is our way of helping you find healthy ways to manage stress, increase focus and move out of the darkness and into a better place.

Perhaps you would feel better talking to another teen. If someone in your family is an alcoholic, would you like to talk to a person near your age with a similar problem? A program called "Alaneen Chat,"[1] a moderated discussion group for teens 13-18 years of age, is available. Teens are "invited to share experience, strength, and hope." In the Chat, you can talk to your peers on your computer or your phone. This service is offered six times a week on differing days.

If you could tell someone about what is really going on, and who is involved without putting yourself or anyone else in danger, then you would feel better by reporting it, knowing that someone would at least investigate, right? A program to do just that, which you can download on your smartphone, is called "Say Something."[2] Developed by a non-profit foundation, called Sandy Hook Promise, the app "allows you to submit secure & anonymous safety concerns to help identify and intervene with at-risk individuals BEFORE they hurt themselves or others." You can report bullying, threats and actions you might feel are dangerous, 24/7. Each message goes straight to a crisis center in Florida, staffed by trained counselors who determine the threat level as dangerous or not dangerous. Where appropriate, calls may be directed to the police department as well as school administrators. They can tell which school neighborhood the call is coming from but <u>nothing personal about the tipster</u>.

If you are feeling depressed and don't want to take medication, new medical procedures are available for depression involving magnetic brainstimulation.[3] Meditation, massage, and even just getting outside and taking a walk can ease a minor depression.

Many alternatives are available to help you get through difficult times, but you will need to reach out to someone for help. Being a teen or young adult isn't easy.

You have a future you don't want to miss, amazing people to meet, places to go, things to see and do. Life is an incredible dynamic adventure, even if it may not seem like it right now. Your future is far bigger than your imagination. Being patient is hard to do and waiting for things unknown and unseen, without anything to give you hope or guidance is even more difficult. However, you can have faith that every great change in life is usually preceeded by a period of collapse and darkness. To become something better than before, to improve and grow requires the awareness and acceptance of what needs changing, the time spent feeling and understanding what it is so you can learn how to release it. This process can be challenging, but you will survive it in time and emerge transformed, like a butterfly from a cocoon.

Many jobs and opportunities have not been imagined yet. Discovering technologies that will allow you to take classes while you sleep, inventing fabric that will clean itself, designing cars that will fly, organizing our world to bring basic food and shelter to everyone, are but a few. You may be the person who finds the cure for cancer, who runs for president and wins, who will be the legendary peacemaker for the planet.

If you feel you need help, close this book right now and reach out. Call 911, contact a trusted adult, or access "Moving Your Mind," "Alaneen Chat," "Say Something," or go to: https://www.connectsafely.org/resources-for-youth-in-crisis/ which lists many other services for help. You can find something, somewhere that will appeal to you.

Be patient with yourself.

Forgive yourself.

You are needed in this world.

Don't miss it.

---

[1] https://al-anon.org/newcomers/teen-corner-alateen/try-an-alateen-chat-meeting/
[2] For more information visit www.saysomething.net #saysomething
[3] https://www.healthline.com/health/depression/repetitive-transcranial-magnetic-stimulation

NOTES

 # FREEDOM IS AN INSIDE JOB

Freedom is the theme of *Breaking Strings*, covering various aspects of freedom and how to obtain them. The book starts with the example of Pinocchio because he wanted freedom from the physical ties to his father. As teens and young adults, you, too, are loosening the physical ties from your parents. You probably want to break more than the physical ties, but also those mental, emotional, and spiritual ties, and think for yourself. That is true freedom.

You may first think of freedom in a physical way. The freedom to travel may come to mind — seeing new cities, states, and countries, or just getting out of the family home. You may think of freedom as attaining something new — that purse, those shoes, a car, a girlfriend or boyfriend. However, true freedom has to do with a feeling, an attitude when you receive what you have wished for. Have you wondered why, say a certain car, would excite one person but not the next? It has nothing to do with the actual car but how a person feels about the car.

So where do these feelings originate? All feelings come from the inside out, independent from outer circumstances. Remember the Disney movie, *Inside Out*? Since they rule our attitudes, our words, and what we do, they control our sense of well-being and freedom, having little to do with anything outer such as our living conditions, our caregivers, our car, our friends or that special friend.

Every moment, we have a key from our feelings about how we want to view our surroundings and circumstances. Sometimes we need to change the outer circumstances. Other times, we just need to change our thoughts and feelings about them. If we view a circumstance as negative, another way to look at it might be to view it as a learning and therefore it can become a positive, and a resolution can occur because balance is restored. The wisdom of the "Serenity Prayer" can be a guide.

> God, grant me the serenity to accept the things I cannot change, the courage to change the things I can, and the wisdom to know the difference.

Our feelings can help stabilize us when we feel ourselves in rough waters, or sometimes even adrift. They are our friends and should always be listened to and not stuffed. If you decide to stuff negative feelings such as hurt, anger, fear, resentment, blame, or a loss, they won't go away, but fester and run your life from your subconscious. Some call these stuffed emotions "pain bodies," "triggers," or "buttons." You may have heard people say "it pushed their button."

True freedom is having no buttons that we allow our outer circumstances to push, yet everyone has these. They are remnants of our defense system we designed to protect ourselves when we were young. Now that you are maturing, they are a hindrance rather than a help. So, is it possible to eliminate one's buttons? Maybe not completely, but if you are aware of them, accept them and are willing to "let them go," you may be able to lessen their effect.

I recommend a book, *Radical Compassion* by Tara Branch, Viking Life Publishers, 2019, which describes RAIN. RAIN is a synonym for the process of how to resolve the buttons that show up in our lives. R stands for recognize. A stands for accept. I stands for investigate. N stands for nurture. The book is easy to read and very clear.

I had a button for the first 35 years of my life that made me afraid of men, so much so I avoided them as much as possible. In my 20s and 30s, I couldn't look a man in the eye. I realized that my mom, because of her life experience, taught me that all men were not to be trusted and could hurt me. When I discovered the cause of my fear was my mom's experience and not my own, I started a practice of looking at men in the eye, just a few a day. I was able to work out of my fear button.

A book written in 2002 by Dr. David Hawkins, M.D. and Ph.D., was the last of his 14 books about consciousness, their levels, and how repressed feelings hinder us. *Letting Go . . . The Pathway to Surrender*, describes various feelings, their levels of consciousness, and the process to let the negative ones go. The book was not written specifically for young people, but it's not difficult to read, has a helpful chart, and is a jewel to understanding levels of feelings, their consequences and resolutions. This process of discovery and letting go is a life-long process.

Freedom is important because it is the prerequisite to love. One cannot truly love until one is free. The experiences we feel that have been negative and cause "buttons," cloud our perception and our decision-making, creating filters we see through. Cleaning those filters is a life-long process. As you are able to resolve each button and see more clearly, you are able to have a more fulfilling life, happier and more at peace.

Step 1: Awareness

Are you aware of any buttons you may have — when "someone made you" angry, sad, hurt?

_____

_____

_____

_____

_____

Step 2: Accept and Release

Can you see to see the fallacy of your button and choose another way to see the incident?

_____

_____

_____

_____

_____

In the following chapters, Pinocchio will give you additional help to clear your filters so that you, too, may become free.

The adventure begins!

NOTES

# TRUTHS AND MISCONCEPTIONS

Truths:

Strings are breaking, that is true. The physical strings that tied you to your parents or caregivers break as you leave home for college, a job or just to be on your own. Even before that, psychological strings break while still at home because you are maturing and starting to think for yourself. You don't completely agree with your parents about everything. This physical and psychological breaking away is natural and needed as you become a young adult. Quite often, starting to think for yourself causes problems at home. Parents may have a difficult time loosening those strings they used to keep you safe while you were growing up.

Pinocchio is featured in this book because he, too, wanted to break away from his parent and be free. He had problems as a puppet of a child who couldn't act, move, or speak until a parent pulled the strings. He grew tired of that and wanted to be real.

Everyone has problems with their parents, some more than others. I'm sure you've heard, "parents do the best they can" and "there is no training for being a parent." These statements are true, but too simplistic, and concepts don't help much when you're in pain because of your parents, foster parents or other family members. They aren't perfect and often create problems because they have issues in their lives they haven't resolved for themselves.

Misconceptions:

There are also misconceptions you developed yourself. In addition to the strings your parents used, you developed some yourself as a young child in order to try to receive love from them.

Wait. This is to alert you that the subject of self-imposed strings is not typical for teens and young adults. It is usually discovered when adults realize they have developed patterns, like addictions to food, to shopping, to money, to acceptance from other people. Searching deeply for the cause of these addictions, one may find these self-imposed strings.

What are these patterns that result from the self-imposed strings? Do you find yourself "introverted?" You may have tried to please your parents by being quiet. "Children should be seen and not heard." Or did you choose to be more of an "extrovert," being talkative and entertaining? Have you chosen to be the "good" boy or girl or the opposite, the "bad," just to get your parents attention? Whatever the case, these self-imposed strings are not the true you, your birthright of being lovable, whole, and free.

Many articles and books have been written on decisions you have made in childhood. If you need to investigate this further, take a look at "Adolescence and the Need to Please Parents,"[1] by Carl E. Pickhard, Ph.D. The article is written for parents, but you may relate to some of his examples.

The strings you developed were a "brilliant strategy" as stated by TJ Woodward in his book, *Conscious Recovery*. You needed these to try to get love from your parents, but even now may be starting to sabotage you. Friends and others may not respond the same and give you feedback like your parents did. These core beliefs you developed as a child may continue to haunt you your entire life unless you become aware of them. Did your caregivers tell you, or did you assume, you were stupid, fat, ugly, bad or unkind? Even if you were called cute, happy, smart or giving, they were labels you may have believed were the "total" you.

From negative judgments, you may have assumed you were this way down deep, so you tried to cover them up. You may have felt you were not good enough, there was something wrong with you, you were truly unlovable. These beliefs may cause you negative reactions like always wanting to be right, to be in control, to feel you are better than, to not be willing to admit you've made a mistake, to name a few. In the case of more positive thoughts, you may have tried to reinforce them. Are you becoming worn out trying to live up to too high a standard, starting to judge others as shallow, have an inflated view of yourself, or being a perfectionist. Either way, you may have looked to others who think of you in those ways, in order to prove to yourself you were right about the misconceptions you have adopted about yourself.

What are three things that you were told, assumed, or decided about yourself when you were young?

1._____

_____

2._____

_____

3._____

_____

How have you tried to hide them (eating, drinking, depression) or tried to reinforce them (over achieving, perfectionism)?

1._____

_____

2._____

_____

3._____

_____

We all have been parent-pleasers and then we started to become the people-pleasers, using the same strategy. At one time, I worked at the front desk of an academic department in a university. When freshmen came in with a need, sometimes they would be mad, sometimes nice. I'd look at the other staff in the department and say, "I wonder if that's the same way they got what they wanted from their parents."

As the author of this book, I'm also a grandmother. I made decisions in my childhood that affected my whole life. My experience with my parents was more a problem of what they didn't do than what they did do. Generally, my parents were loving and supportive, but in my household we were very quiet and seldom talked about anything. My dad seemed depressed and although my mom talked "at me" and "to me," she rarely talked "with me." My dad was into sports and watched them all the time, sometimes with multiple TVs and radios going at the same time. My mom was working either outside or inside the home. We ate dinner on TV trays, watching TV. It seemed like we were all on auto-pilot, like in a trance. I felt invisible in my own home and I made assumptions about who I was and how to receive love. Part of my strategy was to stay unseen.

Attending college was a big shock because I found I had shut down almost completely. I was afraid to talk. By being silent, I was enforcing the only way I knew how to be accepted. Others wanted to know what I thought about things and I had never had discussions like that. I felt very insecure and fearful of any new situation, especially speaking up when in a group of people.

After college, my husband and I worked with an educational foundation and there were many discussion groups. I was petrified to speak up, even to give my name and where I lived. I decided I was going to conquer my fear by starting to say just one thing in the group the next time we met. Then the next time, I said two things, the next time three, then four and so on. I worked myself out of my fear. Currently, I still have trouble expressing myself verbally. I can make a point, but cannot seem to elaborate on it. I am much better at writing because I can take my time and go back and edit. One doesn't have to be proficient at everything.

Everyone has false beliefs from childhood. The key is what you do about them. Even if you had a difficult time as a youth, with courage you can overcome those strings that bind you.

What if you Knew You Were Enough?

- What if you knew that the beliefs that are rolling around in your subconscious mind are not yours?

- What if you knew that your mind unfortunately had been used against you?

- What if I told you that it's not your fault if you have felt abandoned and unloved; unappreciated, discarded, and like you were bad?

- What if you knew it was your right to feel loved?

- What if you knew that your parents, your culture, your faith had a responsibility to rear children being rooted in self-love?

- What if you knew you had a right to dream a different dream than the people who raised you?

- What if you knew that you were never supposed to live in fear?

- What if when you looked around at other children you felt as worthy as you believed they were?

- What if you knew that no matter what you wanted, you could truly have it? What if you knew you even deserved it?

- What if I told you things could be different and you could awaken?

- What if you knew that you were powerful and that within your mind was the key to manifesting a dream worth living?

- What if you knew that in spite of never feeling loved as a child, you came from love, and you can love yourself?

- What if you knew that by learning to observe what is happening in the subconscious mind you can detach from the dogma, the propaganda, the illusions and the dream the subconscious mind did not know it was dreaming?

- What if you knew that you could overcome your childhood programming?

By Lisa A. Romano — Life Coach, Mentor and bestselling author, www.lisaaromano.com

You are an amazing being, coming to this earth with a birthright that is free, open, curious, and loving. You have been handed a garden. It was free at first, but others have planted plants in it. The plants have different needs for water and nutrients and some of them inhibit the others. The plants are demanding and it is not a joy to care for them. It is possible to clear out all those you don't want, the ones that are dying and cause you stress, and plant new ones of your choosing. The garden can become as it was intended in the beginning — open, free, and loving. You can break the strings that have inhibited your garden, your birthright.

Our thoughts are determined by what is planted in our garden, molding what we do and what we become. As a young person, with every decision you make, you are forming who you are and will be. You are writing your own autobiography. Our decisions determine how we feel about ourselves — our self-worth. I remember telling my children one's self-worth is one of the most important things they have. Is cheating on an exam worth setting a course to be a deceitful person? Is lying to your parents worth molding yourself as a liar? Is taking drugs worth damaging your mind and body?

There is a saying you may have heard, "What goes around comes around." It's true. It's a psychological principle that whatever you give out comes back to you. One example is when you express your anger toward someone, often you get an angry response back. It's also called The Law of Attraction. Several books have been written on this subject, including those by Esther and Jerry Hicks.[2]

How you feel about something is very important. It's possible to view anything as either a learning opportunity or as harmful and negative. Actually, the incident is neutral. It will not be what happens to you in life, but how you feel about it. You can learn from it or choose to be a victim.

As you read *Breaking Strings*, you may find answers and keys to the problems you face either from the text in this workbook or from feelings and ideas that pop into your mind while reading.

Included in this book are milestones you will no doubt face in life, so you can handle them — rather than letting them handle you.

Breaking Strings, Pinocchio Tells The Truth About Being Free, is intended to offer you help with your parents and guide you through other problems you will face in life — schooling, socialization, choosing a career, difficult people, and tough situations. To be truly free, in addition to breaking the physical strings from Geppetto, Pinocchio had to become mentally, emotionally, and spiritually free, by becoming "brave, truthful, and unselfish." It's a challenge for you, too, as you encounter life. A self-challenge.

---

[1] https://www.psychologytoday.com/us/blog/surviving-your-childs-adolescence/201404/adolescence-and-the-need-please-parents

[2] The most well known is *The Law of Attraction: The Basic Teachings of Abraham* by Esther and Jerry Hicks, #5 in a series of 7, Hay House, Inc.

NOTES

LESSONS FROM A WOODEN BOY

In an interesting way, Pinocchio's desire to be real, without someone else pulling his strings, is similar to yours. You can make decisions for yourself now and don't want anyone else, especially your parent, "pulling your strings." The inborn, natural thing to do in becoming an adult is to test the limits and break free of the "strings." This stage may even be harder on your parents than on you because often they have used those strings to keep you from harm and guide you. Now they have difficulty cutting those strings.

We move through four quadrants in our lives — physical, mental, emotional, and spiritual. As a baby in the physical quadrant, you needed someone to help you physically and keep you safe. As a young person, you are in the mental stage (school), moving into the emotional (love, lust, gratitude). Often, the spiritual quadrant is entered later in life when the business of life has slowed down, when the children are out of the house and on their own, when as adults you are retired. However, you may be interested in the spiritual earlier if you start asking those spiritual questions — Who am I? Why was I born? How do I find meaning in life? What is life really all about? Does God exist, and if so what does He/She/It do and not do?

Where you are in the quadrants has only partially to do with age. You never completely move out of one into another because all of them are interconnected. They are with you all the time. What is important is having broken the strings and having learned the lessons in each stage.

You probably know others of your age who seem like "old souls" and understand the spiritual quadrant. On the other hand, some adults don't have a clue about much of anything. If they do not become aware of the spiritual, they can become negative and disillusioned later in life.

Your parents may also feel someone else is pulling their strings, be it their parents, their supervisor at work, their friends, financial institutions, the government, the armed services or many other facets in life. This can be the cause of a great deal of anger in adults, whether they are aware of it or not. When the event actually happened is irrelevant. The parent or friend could be dead or not. The problem at work may have been two jobs ago.

In our society, what does it mean to be mature? Does it only have to do with physical age? Are there any standards? We face different age limits for:

1. voting,

2. being able to drive,

3. enlisting in the armed services,

4. movie tickets,

5. buying alcohol.

Rather than defining maturity by physical age, another definition for you to consider is:

1. the ability to entertain yourself

2. to entertain another person

3. to entertain an idea.

There will be many ideas in this book you will have the opportunity to entertain. To accept them or not is your choice, since you are an individual with free will. An important life issue for you will be to decide things for yourself, not just accept another's opinion or experience as your own. Also, be aware, as you read, of any physical reactions you may have to what you are reading. Some get chills when what they have read rings true to them.

True maturity is the ability to think beyond:

1. what you want for yourself,

2. your pride,

3. your identity,

4. your ethnicity,

5. your country.

True maturity is an understanding of the oneness of all things and people. It is a state desired and achieved by few but is one that is an ingredient of true love and freedom.

Pinocchio wanted freedom from Geppetto pulling his strings. The concepts of freedom and free will have molded the history of the world – freedom of speech, freedom to live where we choose, freedom of religious choice, freedom of whom to marry. The American Revolution was a revolt over the strings the British Empire held over the colonies. The OCCUPY riots in September and October of 2011 in the United States were examples of adults protesting the strings that financial people and the wealthy have pulled over the middle and lower classes. BREXIT was an example of the

United Kingdom wanting to break the strings from the European Union. The Me Too movement was the beginning of the strings breaking from sexual harassment and sexual assault. The Black Lives Matter movement is a revolt over the strings pulled by the U.S. police force over African Americans.

All of us have a different definition of freedom. For Pinocchio it meant freedom from his dad's strings and being able to make his own choices. For us, it may mean making a "decent" living so there will be fewer monetary worries. For others, it may mean travel. Some may feel freedom is staying out of jail. Maybe freedom involves controlling our environment. Others may feel freedom is having those emotional strings broken from many sources – parents, friends, neighbors, jobs, status.

What is life all about, anyway? Could it be like a test? If so, what are the answers and what is the reward? Does doing well on the test mean we'd control our environment, control others or just ourselves? In a

deeper sense, the test is not really about controlling the outer world, but having control of the inner world.

In the past, I had thought the worst thing that could happen to me was to be in jail and lose my freedom. But then I read Viktor Frankl's book, *Man's Search for Meaning*, and it changed my idea about what freedom really was. He was incarcerated in a Nazi concentration camp. In spite of this, he was able to find meaning there and not be in despair. They could not control his mind and his attitude. Inner freedom is all about feeling. We are designed to live with a feeling of abundance, love, hope, inner peace, non-judgment, inclusiveness, thankfulness, gratitude, and forgiveness. We are made to not just survive but to thrive.

That is what life is all about — to be able to transcend everything that happens to us (what we consider negative) so we can have inner peace. Accepting and being at peace, no matter what happens to us, is truly possible. The key is . . . not what happens, but how we interpret it. Neale Donald Walsch tells us, "It's not how many terrible things we have in our lives, but the number of times we call them terrible."

So, now you may identify a little more with Pinocchio. But how does one break those strings and live with a feeling of freedom? How is it possible to see the positive side in every act and situation? Some say true maturity and the goal in living are to not get stuck in the negative (anger, hurt, resentment) in our lives, but to find a way to move out of that. One way is to look for what you can learn from the experience.

In the following chapters, you will discover there are levels of understanding (maybe even your parents don't know) that will help you to not only understand them and why they have the problems they do, but also how that understanding will help you grow into a mature and self-reliant individual. In essence, for you to be free, too, like Pinocchio.

NOTES

AN INKLING AND A NAGGING FROM A CRICKET

There's another main character in the Pinocchio story besides Pinocchio and Geppetto — the cricket named Jiminy. In the original version of the story by Carlo Collodi (1883), Jiminy was killed by Pinocchio and then returns as a ghost. In the Disney version however (1940), Jiminy goes with Pinocchio on his journeys as a cricket. In either case, remember fairy tales are myths, stories that have hidden psychological meanings. So, who or what does Jiminy Cricket represent?

Some say it's our conscience, that part of us (our little voice), that helps us determine right from wrong. There can be even a deeper meaning, more than help with right and wrong, because the conscience is an active part of Pinocchio's higher self. The higher self is often called the self with a big "S." You may not have heard of a person's higher self.

You probably have heard of the ego, the self with the small "s," which is an aspect that most commonly rules us. The ego is concerned with what is mine, what I want, what I do. It's all me, me, me. Our higher self is focused on the concern for the whole, for all people, with giving and sharing. The higher self is the key to becoming "brave, truthful and unselfish," the qualities needed to become a real boy, in the Pinocchio story. The idea is not to get rid of the ego. It's not an inherently negative or bad part of us. A political psychologist, Thomas Hobbes, in *De Cive* (The Citizen), talked about the ego using the term "self-interest." He believed as we come to acknowledge and understand how our egos work, we'll uncover and desire to better develop our higher self.

We're not born with an ego but as a young child when we see we're different from others, we begin to form an identity. A separation from others begins to form. As we have life experiences that we feel cause us pain, the ego may take over our higher self, because it feels our survival is threatened. We become afraid, we hide, we protect, we put others down to make ourselves feel better. We try to get "them" before "they" can get us.

In the Pinocchio story, Pinocchio escapes from his father, Geppetto, desiring to become a real boy. His higher self, Jiminy, goes with him to try to save him from what his ego desires. Pinocchio had several adventures where he was tested in becoming truthful, brave, and unselfish. Pinocchio's egotistical ways caused him to lie, which show up physically with his nose growing longer and longer. Our egotistical ways don't make us physically change on the outside like Pinocchio, but changes us inside — what we think about others and ourselves. Only following one's ego can lead to a lack of self-respect for ourselves, leading us to having negative thoughts and actions toward others.

When you enter your professional life, you may have major experiences when your higher self and ego will be tested. Will you construct that building to the correct specifications? Or will you cut costs using substandard construction materials to gain a bigger profit? As a government official, will you serve your country or will you be more concerned about being re-elected? As a firefighter, will you overcome your survival instincts to enter that building to save another? As an investment counselor, will you succumb to insider trading to "make a killing" for yourself?

The inklings and naggings occur on a day-by-day basis. Will you eat what is right for your body, or will you always give in to something sugary or alcoholic? Will you go out of your way to help a friend or stranger, even if it will inconvenience you a bit?

The sooner you begin to control your ego and uncover your higher self, the less chance the negative effects of the ego can take over and rule your life. You probably know people who have a strong, negative, ego personality and the damage that creates.

I'm sure you're already aware of Jiminy, your higher self. He is always present, wanting to help you on your journey, as he did with Pinocchio. Be aware of how he gives you a inkling and a nagging as you read this book.

How and when do you experience Jiminy?

_____

_____

_____

_____

_____

NOTES

IS SCHOOL A PROBLEM FOR YOU?
by SJ Farry

Hi, I'm SJ. I graduated from high school in 2019. My life through school was non-traditional. No matter what kind of schooling you're in, I hope my story will resonate with you.

As an elementary school student, I was, for lack of a better word, a try-hard. I pushed myself to be a part of everything that was offered to me. I played an instrument, got all my homework done on time, raised my hand for every question and always spoke up if there was an opportunity to correct the teacher.

By the sixth grade, I had a 10-year-plan laid out. I knew who I was, what I wanted to be, and that I had a bright future ahead of me. However, this plan was about to come to a crashing halt.

Many people work well in the 30-to-a-classroom system. They thrive in traditional schools. They enjoy the social life, sports, music, theatre, leadership opportunities, and everything else that public school has to offer. For a large part of my life, I was this person. I wanted everything life and school had to offer and thought I could do it all. So I did.

I worked and I worked and I worked. Sixth, seventh, and eighth grade were filled with band, "accelerated" and "advanced" classes, after-school volunteering, and a nanny jobs in the evenings. But no matter how much I filled my life with what I expected to want or was expected to want, it wasn't enough. My life was full, but my heart was empty.

The best way I can describe my middle school self is like looking into a broken mirror. In reality, I was looking at me, but not all of me. And the parts of me that were there didn't quite line up right. I had pushed myself so hard, my mental tank ran out of fuel.

I didn't have the energy to keep going and knew if I kept pushing I would just keep breaking. I needed time to heal, but how can you when everything else in your life keeps moving with or without you? Later in my life, I understood there were names (and solutions) for the things I was feeling, but at the moment I felt alone.

By eighth grade, the hopelessness had caught up with me. My 10-year plan had gone down the drain. Depression and anxiety had filled its place. I was no longer happy and I couldn't remember the last time I had been happy. I didn't want to eat, didn't want to breathe. I didn't want to wake up. Most of all, I didn't want anybody to know about it.

How do you tell someone you're through with living? How do you tell some that you, a 13-year-old can't do it anymore? This life thing isn't for you. You're over it.

I had a decision to make. Either I was going to find a way to make life slow down a little bit, or I was going to keep getting dragged behind it like a water skier who can't figure out how to stand up. I knew staying in the traditional public school system wasn't going to work for me. I needed to find another option.

This started with opening up to my parents. I hadn't been talking with them about my feelings, so conversations like these were hard to have. Even though sometimes it didn't feel like it, I look back and realize how supportive and understanding my parents were through the whole transition and healing process. I had walled up so many things in my soul and when I started opening up it was like a dam bursting. I hate to admit this, but my poor parents became my emotional punching bag during this time of struggle. I can never repay them for that. I am forever grateful for their continued patience and love. Once I explained myself things began to move. Within a few months, I was out of the traditional school system, in therapy, and had left most of the friends I had held onto for years.

With the support of my parents, I went in search of a non-traditional high school. Each of my older brothers had attended non-traditional high schools, so I knew they existed, I just didn't know where or which one was right for me.

I found my answer on the edge of my middle school campus in a small building, about half the size of a traditional school hallway. I soon understood that tiny building to be the home base for a high school independent study program. Accredited as a traditional school, this program would allow me to attend a few classes at my local comprehensive high school, some at the local community college, some online, and some on my own.

Complicated as it sounds, this arrangement was my saving grace. I was able to take the time I needed to go to therapy, to heal my heart, to once again love my life and myself. Contrary to what we are told by countless media influencers and politicians, I found no "one size fits all" schooling solution, and "no answer" applies to everyone. If you feel a similar way about a traditional school as I did, I encourage you to seek out alternatives, and not give up for you can always find a way out and a way to succeed, even if it's outside of the box.

If you are struggling to pinpoint what changes (if any) could benefit your educational experience, take this quiz to find some insights.

Are these statements True or False for you?

T F I am happy at school most of the time.

T F I sometimes have anxiety about school projects and papers. However, not every day, and that does not affect my ability to function regularly.

T F I have hope for the future.

T F The amount of sadness I feel is normal.

T F When I am sad, the cause isn't always rooted in school or schoolwork.

T F I am content with my life, I don't often find myself longing for more.

T F I can imagine myself continuing happily in the school system I'm currently in.

T F I am not frustrated/frazzled by the social atmosphere around me.

Your answers to these questions may help you understand how your current schooling situation is affecting your mental health. If your schooling experience so far has been an overall positive experience, be grateful for that. Enjoy your time in school and love the opportunities you have now, for they will not be available forever.

However, if you are someone who feels your current schooling situation is not what you need, do not give up. Hope will come with time and as you try to discover the right schooling fit for you. Learn to say "no" to things that are simply an excess in your life. (This is not a natural skill. It will take practice and time.) Be patient with yourself.

Along with homeschooling, online schools, charter or private schools, often public school districts in the United States have non-traditional educational options that are available but not well promoted.

Find out what your local school district has by going to their website (or possibly even the district office). Don't settle for sadness. You can be happy, however it may require some searching in unexpected places.

Remember, a high school diploma should be of the utmost importance to you. Having a diploma is an important rung on the ladder of life, and the lack of one will be a wall to those who did not put in the required time and effort. You will be rewarded in life for all you accomplish in school. It's important to invest in yourself.

Good luck, my brothers and sisters.

* * * *

A note from Patricia McCulley, author. What a success story. SJ is currently a freshman at Brigham Young University.

A note from Pinocchio. Dad wanted me to go to school when I left, but I didn't. Instead, I was lured by fame and fortune, which almost cost me my life and that of my father's.

NOTES

SEX AND SEXUALITY

Pinocchio did not have a problem with his sex or sexuality because he wasn't a human. However, as an evolved human being, you may find the topics of sexuality, gender, and gender identity confusing. The subject is more complicated than in the past when male or female, straight or gay were the limits of possibilities.

Assigned Designation:

It's now illegal to ask on job applications about one's "assigned designation at birth" of male or female, unless the job has specific qualifications for one sex or the other. And what if you're an "intersex," have XXY chromosomes, or sexual body parts of both sexes?

Gender Identity:

Gender has to do with an individual's social roles, or how they are supposed to act, especially according to their culture and society. For a long time, men and women were supposed to act in very specific ways. These roles are dramatically shifting.

Gender identity has to do with sexual orientation, how people feel about their gender. This is where the real complexity begins. Some internet sites state there are as many as 17 sexual orientations. Just ask Google if you're interested in finding out more. You're able to take a test to find out which one you may be.

Even Planned Parenthood has stepped in to help you navigate the maze by explaining these topics further. Their website is: https://www.plannedparenthood.org/learn/teens/all-about-sex-gender-and-gender-identity

It's complicated, but without our sexuality, the human race would not continue. We need it to produce future generations, so it's naturally built-in, just like with all living things. We also can move through experiencing lust to understanding what true love can be — the love of a pet, a partner, the Earth, the world and all people in it. Our true nature is to love and our sexuality is one way to get us there.

As we grow up, we become more and more aware of our sexuality. An investigation may start early in life with self-exploration or "playing doctor" with a childhood friend, which is all healthy.

However, sometimes others take advantage of a child, which can lead to lifelong damage. Hurtful incidents that happen as a child may be remembered one's whole life. I am a grandmother and I still have some anxiety from an incident that happened to me as a seven-year-old by a man, I'll call him Charlie, who rented a room in our house. He became a family friend and was my babysitter when my parents went out for the evening. At the time, I didn't tell anyone he abused me because I thought it was my fault and I feared I was pregnant. When I found out about two years later how babies were really conceived, I lost the fear of pregnancy, but the guilt remained until I was a teenager. Then, I realized Charlie was the one to blame, not me. My mom found out about Charlie when I was about sixteen. I had a huge reaction when she told me the family was going to visit Charlie that summer. I told her I was not going and she asked why. She told me not to tell my dad, or he'd kill Charlie.

A study stating what science says about adverse experiences and our health was printed in the "High Desert PULSE" magazine in Central Oregon, Spring/Summer, 2018.

> A landmark study in 1998 found that individuals who experienced one or more of ten types of traumatic experiences in childhood had a higher risk of physical and mental health problems their entire life. Percent experiencing problems having had adverse childhood experiences —
>
> ABUSE:
> Psychological abuse 11%, Physical 28%, Sexual 21%,
>
> HOUSEHOLD DYSFUNCTION:
> Substance abuse 27%, Parents separated/divorced 23%, Mental illness 17%, Domestic violence 13%, Criminal behavior 8%,
>
> NEGLECT:
> Emotional 15%, Physical 10%. . . . When you have trauma you feel like a tiger is chasing you — you act like a tiger is chasing you even if it isn't, just because it did at one time.

If you have had a traumatic experience, talk to an adult you trust. When the experience is hidden, the negative memories can last your whole lifetime, as it did with me.

Senate Hearings:

During the 2019 Senate hearings on the potential appointment of Brett Kavanaugh to the United States Supreme Court, Dr. Christine Blasey Ford gave her account of the sexual assault she experienced by him when she was a teenager. As she was testifying, I got upset again. I realized, 73 years later, remnants of the abuse I experienced still bothered me. To free myself, I talked out those remnants with a trusted female friend. I urge you to have courage to find someone to talk to now so you don't have the incident lingering for the rest of your life.

Sexual Partners:

Unprotected sex is a concern whenever you start having sex. I remember when our son and daughter were in their early years of high school, my husband and I offered to buy them a car if they could make it through high school without having any sexual partners. Our plan did not work. They turned us down. One was too interested. The other, well, the offer came too late. So we decided protection should be the next subject of a family discussion.

Unprotected Sex:

The consequences of unprotected sex can be grave in your life and the life of others. Sexually transmitted illnesses such as gonorrhea and herpes are still around. And now with AIDS, one encounter can lead to life-long sickness and death. You never really know what sexual partners your lover has had.

Unprotected (and sometimes even protected) sex always has the possibility of an unplanned pregnancy. As a female, there comes a plethora of difficult options: keeping and raising the baby yourself, having a relative or friend raise the baby, giving the baby up for adoption, or having an abortion. These all have lifelong drawbacks for you and the child. Guilt, fear, and regret can all be present at the same time and keep you tied to the past, rather than living in the present. For the child, the issue of abandonment can leave lifelong scars. And when those children reach adulthood, they may spend most of their lives searching, sometimes in vain, for their biological parents.

As a male, if you happen to get someone pregnant, similar negative consequences arise. Again guilt, fear, and regret can keep you tied to the past and prevented from living in the present. So many questions arise. What will the mother do with the child? How can you come to terms with her decision? When the child grows up, will he or she come looking for you? Will that disrupt your life then?

You can avoid most negative outcomes if you are responsible and use contraception. Or — you can abstain, which is a healthy choice. Choosing to remain chaste does not mean you don't date. Being physically active on your dates like walking, jogging, hiking, biking, swimming, bowling, miniature golf, and avoidance of late nights and drinking at parties can lead to a safe, fun, and memorable middle school, high school and college experience.

Pornography:

Especially for you guys, but also sometimes for girls, pornography can become a challenging problem. As you probably know, today almost anyone can get free access to pornography on his or her smartphone.

Arthur Paull, Licensed Clinical Social Worker, a psychotherapist specializing in teens that have sexual behavior problems, tells us, "Many teens become addicted to pornography. This addiction can actually limit their ability to have healthy romantic relationships with other teens with whom they're attracted. Also there are many really unhealthy illegal forms of pornography, such as child porn."

If you feel you may be becoming addicted to porn or are watching deviant, or other unhealthy types of pornography, reach out to someone you trust and ask for help. This can be the first step toward having a healthier sex life. Also, if this problem is interfering with your life, seek help from a licensed therapist. In addition, there are now community-based groups that can help you with these problems in a confidential manner.

Whatever your orientation, remember your sexuality is a beautiful, wonderful thing, to be protected and explored with responsibility. If you have questions or doubts, choosing to be open with a trusted adult can make these years of potential mistakes and frustrations run a whole lot smoother.

Have Courage:

Be honest and true to yourself. Your adult self will thank you. Pinocchio had it easy.

What decisions have you made about your sexuality?

_____

_____

_____

_____

_____

_____

_____

_____

NOTES

DECISIONS, DECISIONS, DECISIONS

Pinocchio was plagued by decisions when he left Geppetto. Most of the decisions he made got him into trouble because he didn't listen to Jiminy Cricket, his higher self. Instead of obeying his father and going to school, he sold his schoolbook to see a puppet show and barely escaped being used as firewood.

Pinocchio was tempted by greed in another decision. Instead of being grateful for the money he had, he was swindled by some strangers to go to Dupeland, where he was told he could get rich without hard work and earning money honestly. He spent some time in jail, and almost ended up turning into a donkey.

Not until Pinocchio risked his own life to save his dad from the belly of a whale was he acting in a "brave, truthful and unselfish" manner. He had learned some life lessons from his decisions as will you as you mature.

Now you have to make decisions, maybe more than you wanted. Your parents used to make them for you. Now you're making them for yourself. This is what you wanted — to have more freedom to be yourself — just like Pinocchio. Some decisions are somewhat easy. But you know, some are more complex and will involve forks in the road, which will make major impacts in your life.

Some decisions you are making are conscious. Some are unconscious, ones that were programmed when you were little, as we mentioned in Chapter 2. They were needed then. You were learning how to please someone to get love, and how to protect yourself from what you considered harmful. As you mature, breaking those strings from your parents involves making conscious more of those unconscious decisions in life.

Here are four of the more complex decisions that will form the path your life will take. They may be conscious for you already. The four decisions are:

1. To Give or To Take,

2. To Go With the Flow or Against It,

3. To Love or To Fear, and

4. To Have Power or To Be a Victim

These decisions will make a major difference in your life. Will you have inner peace or turmoil, understanding or stress? Will you have compassion or be judgmental toward others?

Decision #1: To Give or To Take

The first of these four decisions is regarding service to others or being self-involved. This doesn't mean you don't fulfill your own needs. You absolutely do. If you don't take care of yourself, you have nothing to give.

Don't go into shock. You don't have to go into the ministry. This has to do with an attitude. Do you think only about yourself, or do you consider others? Oprah Winfrey in the on-line presentation hosted by Facebook to high school seniors and college graduating classes of 2020 called the classes "to consider what their 'essential service' in this world will be . . . "[1] She asked graduates to contemplate how they will use their own passions to benefit those around them.

Your attitudes determine the actions you take. Most patterns start in early childhood. When you were young, did you give some of your allowance to charity, do volunteer work, be kind to others? Even if you didn't have this experience, to give or take has to do with the quality of your heart. Do you feel we are all brothers and sisters on this planet and need to help and encourage each other, or would you rather be alone and serve only yourself most of the time?

Through giving, we experience love. Neale Donald Walsch, an American author of the series, *Conversations with God*, shares:

> ... that love is not what you want, it is what you are. It is very important to not get these two confused. If you think that love is what you want, you will go searching for it all over the place. If you think love is what you are, you will go sharing it all over the place. The second approach will cause you to find what the searching will never reveal. Yet you cannot give love in order to get it. Doing that is as much as saying you do not now have it. And statement will, of course, be your reality. No, you must give love because you have it to give. In this will you experience your own possession of it.

To know that love is what you are, you have to have self-love. Self-love is not being selfish. Selfish is taking something away from others. Many books have been written on self-love, but in essence, it is accepting yourself as you are. We are not perfect and all of us have things we don't like about ourselves. Learning to forgive ourselves is key. Having self-love in itself is a life work.

Give three examples of how you experience love of self.

1._____

_____

_____

2._____

_____

_____

3._____

_____

Give three examples where you see self-love is needed.

1._____

_____

_____

2._____

_____

_____

3._____

_____

Give three examples of where you're giving to others.

1._____

_____

_____

2._____

_____

_____

3._____

_____

_____

Give three examples of ways you can improve giving to others.

1._____

_____

_____

2._____

_____

_____

3._____

_____

Decision #2: To Go with the Flow or Against It

You've heard "go with the flow." The children's rhyme, which you know from when you were a kid, goes, "Row, row, row your boat, gently down the stream . . ." The most important words here are "gently" and "down." Do you have times when you feel you are rowing vigorously upstream and going nowhere? Have you ever realized you were being "stubborn?" Going against the flow can lead to stress in your life, not only causing you emotional pain and suffering, but also major havoc with your body, which can lead to many forms of disease, including heart disease and cancer.

"Going with the flow" is being flexible when something doesn't go your way. Ask, "Is this really such a big deal?" If I'm given lemons, can I make lemonade rather than wanting something different like orange juice? Almost all my life I resisted the flow of having straight hair. I wanted curly hair. After a lifetime of perms, I decided to go with the flow and chose styles to complement my straight hair.

It may be difficult at first to move from, "I don't like this" (a resistance) to an attitude of, "What can I do about this now?" (a creative response). We have not been taught this flexibility at school and perhaps not by our parents. This change in thinking is one of life's continual exercises, but with your awareness and some practice, this manner will become easier over time.

What would it mean for you to accept change as a friend and go with the flow. Change is a constant, but more about that later, because it's a very important "universal principle."

Can you think of three examples where you might be resisting something or someone? What would a more accepting attitude be? Notice how you feel in each instance.

RESISTING　　　　　　　　FLOWING/ACCEPTING

1._____

_____

_____

2._____

_____

_____

3._____

_____

Going with the flow or against it are not real opposites as with the other three types of decisions. There are times when it's not advisable to go with the flow. Those are times when you decide the flow is going in a different direction than you want to go. Those are times when you want to be your own person and decide it's not wise to go along with the crowd. I'm sure you have had the courage to face this already.

There are times when you decide you'll not be bound by the strings being held by your friends, when you want to be free, like Pinocchio. Some examples might be — leaving your friend group when they do something you don't want to do, saying No when everyone else is saying Yes, not agreeing with an opinion you don't believe in just to fit in. These decisions are ageless because we all make these choices daily throughout our lives.

What are three times when you went against the flow and felt better because of it?

1._____

_____

2._____

_____

_____

3._____

_____

_____

Decision #3: To Love or To Fear

A common belief is that the opposite of love is hate. But when you look deeper, the opposite of love is fear, not hate, because hate is caused by fear.

Consider this. When you hate someone, look to see if there might be fear involved. For example, do you dislike someone at school? Perhaps you think that person may hurt you in some way? When they do something better than you, do you feel it belittles and hurts you?

Do you want to live in fear of others or understand them

and get along? This attitude occurs each time you meet a new person, and may happen in an instant. You've probably experienced an instant feeling of like or dislike when you first meet someone. It's a gut feeling. If you fear someone of another ethnicity, what about learning a little about their culture or trying to get to know someone like that.

If you hate/dislike a situation, there is the fear you won't like the consequences it may bring. You may hate spiders because you fear their poison will harm you, or perhaps you just don't like being scared and out of control.

The basis of fear is a lack of acceptance and understanding. When you fear something, learn more about it. Some things you should avoid because they could harm you. Some things not.

Until I was about 30-years-old, I had a fear of snakes. When I was close to something, my mom used to say, "If it was a snake it would've bit you." That didn't help. So I decided to learn about snakes and find out which ones were poisonous and lived where I did. I learned I needed to avoid rattlesnakes, but not other native snakes in California.

That information kept me from dying, literally. I was out fly-fishing in the middle of a river and, without looking, I put my hand back on a log to keep my balance. A snake just happened to be on that log. It bit me and went back into a little hole. I could see its head. It didn't have a triangle-shaped head, so it was not a rattlesnake, only a harmless garter snake, so I wasn't fearful. If I didn't know about snakes, I could've panicked, and lost my footing in that river

What are three examples where you dislike someone or something? Can you discover the underlying fear?

DISLIKE   FEAR

1._____

_____

_____

2._____

_____

_____

3._____

_____

The opposite of fear is Love. Love is strong and freeing. I'm not talking about romantic love, but a caring type of love. Love gives you the freedom to be responsive and creative vs. being restrictive and frozen in action, which is what fear brings. Watch out for fear. Fear can harm your body in many ways, from anxiety to stress, and can lead to diseases like arthritis and cancer.

Decision #4: To Have Power or To Be a Victim

You will also be faced with the choice of having power in your life or being a victim. Another way to say this is of being powerful or powerless. Do you want to be "in control" and come into your own power, or have things "happen to you," pulled by strings from other people and situations, a puppet like Pinocchio.

You can live your whole life and not realize you're giving away your power. To help, here are some instances that may seem familiar.

Victim attitudes occur when you react with anger, hate, or perhaps fear when another person says or does something you don't like. You can either be "stuck" in those feelings or you can see they are your own feelings and change them.

If someone puts you down in front of your friends, instead of feeling resentful, you could wonder about how his morning went. Perhaps, he'll only feel better about himself if he puts someone else down. The problem is his and has nothing to do with you.

It's common to say, "He hurt my feelings." In this instance, you have decided to give away your power vs. seeing your own responsibility and saying, "I felt hurt when he did that." Now you can change how you feel about that. The distinction is subtle, but this is an issue of 1) power, 2) who's in control, and 3) if it can be resolved.

A victim/powerless attitude happens every time you blame someone. You give away your power. You feel someone is doing something to you with a harmful intent. When you blame, you hurt yourself more than the other person. You get stuck in negative emotions such as hate, anger, resentment, and regret. You can stay stuck there forever, if you'd like, or you can forgive and move on with your life.

Feeling powerless can be at home, school, work, even while driving. That's the cause of "road rage" when you feel another driver has done something to you personally. Being in control is to view the instance with an objective attitude.

"Hm-m, I wonder why he did that?" "Maybe he's stressed." "He must have had a bad morning."

I've realized when I'm angry or hurt by a situation or person, it's because I don't like what happened. I'm resisting the reality that it happened. How crazy is that? What do I do now to move on?

Being in control is to understand whatever happens to you can be viewed as a life lesson to learn from, not as a victim of the situation. With this attitude, you'll be wiser as you grow older, because wisdom is gained from learning as you are living, and has nothing to do with how old you are.

Give three examples where you felt like a victim (blame/hurt feelings). What would a more powerful attitude be?

VICTIM/POWERLESS	CONTROL/POWERFUL

1._____

_____

2._____

_____

3._____

_____

You can decide right now to base your life on Giving, Flexibility, Love, Power or you can choose the opposites of Taking, Inflexibility, Fear, and Victimization.

Start by being aware when any of these four attitudes happen as you live each day. These are major life decisions and if you understand them at your age, you'll be giving yourself a huge advantage as you grow older. You'll be able to see them coming and won't be caught off guard. By putting these concepts into practice, you'll be able to build that life of heaven (on Earth), inner peace, compassion, and happiness. In Pinocchio's terms, you can be "brave, truthful and unselfish." You can be free.

Most of us were not given this type of clear information by our parents. It's a whole new evolution in psychology your parents possibly never had. Now's the time to change your subconscious habits you developed as a child. You've outgrown them. Break those strings like Pinocchio did.

---

[1]"Oprah tells Class of 2020 to create a more just world," Bay Area News Group, Star Report, A2, May 17, 202

NOTES

 # TO TRUST OR NOT TO TRUST

Pinocchio had a difficult time finding whom to trust. He met many scoundrels who tried to take advantage of him, and they did. We all struggle to find out whom and what is trustworthy. We start out with our parents and learn some lessons there and then, as we get out into the big wide world, we too meet scoundrels.

What is reality? "Fake News" and "Alternative Facts" are repeated almost daily.

WUMO © 2017 WulfmMorgenthaler, Reprinted with permission of ANDREWS MCMEEL SYNDICATION. All rights reserved.

On television news programs, it depends on which channel we watch as to what is being fed to us as truth. Often we want to trust the thoughts of others, yet, if we think of other's statements as opinions rather than truth, knowing they too see through filters, we may be able to distinguish those who are trustworthy or those who are scoundrels. One key is what is the source of their information.

Have you been searching for what is true? In this chapter, we'll explore the categories of what is suspect and what is trustworthy. You want to entrust your life to something or someone who is reliable and trustworthy. But what or who is that? Have your parents always spoken the truth? Is what you can count on always there? Does what you believe to be the truth ever change?

Some problems with trust come because of misunderstandings. The earliest problem I can remember with my parents started when I was about three-years-old. My parents didn't mean to tell me an untruth, but I thought something different than what they meant. When I received money for Christmas or birthdays, my mom told me I should put the gifts in the bank, and they would keep them for me. The money was so beautiful — crisp bills and shiny coins. I was willing to give them up, for the time being. When I was about seven-years-old and wanted to see that beautiful money again and to spend some of it, I was disappointed I didn't get back the exact same pieces I'd put in the bank, the crisp bills and shiny coins. I thought they had kept them for me in some kind of a box at the bank and nobody touched it.

You may have or had examples of misunderstandings with your parents.

_____

_____

_____

_____

_____

Why don't your parents tell the truth all the time? Do they know the truth or have they been mislead? Do they have strings, like Pinocchio, that bind them to their parents' ideas, to what they watch on TV, to the opinions of their friends, to what they read in books and in newspapers? I remember when I entered the university, I would say "they" said something. A friend asked me who "they" were and I was not sure, but it's a term my parents used.

What we see may not always be true. That's why the saying "looking through rose colored glasses" came about. Another way to look at this is we all see through filters, even as a young person. Developed in early childhood, filters have built up through our lifetime.

Everyone thinks they see the truth, but our eyes can deceive us. We can be well intentioned, but many times what we see or hear is not the whole truth. Criminologists tell us eyewitnesses are among the least reliable for crime scene facts. Court cases can take a turn when eyewitnesses disagree on what they have seen. Did she have her glasses on when she saw that man across the street? Was he tired or inebriated when he saw the accident? Had he a grudge from his past that influenced his perception of the robbery? Was that a real gun in the mugger's hand?

Have you seen a glacier or a picture of one that has had a portion fall off into the ocean? Did you see the blue color inside where the portion fell off? Did you conclude that maybe the inside of glaciers are blue in color? They aren't. The blue color exists for a short time because the temperature right then in that area is still very cold. When it warms, the blue color will disappear. The glacier is really all colors, absorbs all colors, except blue when the temperature is still too cold. Sometimes we make snap judgments about things that may not be true.

Camel Caravan, Wadi Mitan ©George Steinmetz

What do you see in this picture above? Camels in the desert? Yes and No. In this aerial photo, most apparent are the large dark shapes. However, the large dark shapes are really the shadows of the camels. One has to look closely to see that the real camels are the little objects at the feet of the shadows. This example is to remind us not to be too quick to evaluate and judge. What one sees at first in a situation or thought, may not be the true or complete reality.

What You Can't Count On

Here are some areas that may lead you astray.

1. Physical things

You can't count on anything you see or touch. Why? Because everything physical decays. Buildings, streets, furniture will decay, although we may not see it in our lifetime. All living animals, birds, insects have a certain lifespan. Our beloved animals will get old and leave us. I cherish every moment I have with my beloved cats, knowing they may get sick or get lost at any time. We can't count on our bodies to retain their youth. This may be especially challenging for athletes when they eventually lose their flexibility and strength. As we live and sustain injuries, our health will change, and often we will have a tendency to gain weight because of inactivity. Often these issues about our bodies can be difficult to accept.

2. Wealth

Can you count on money for happiness or security? Money brings a freedom to buy things, go places, do things, but often you can be unhappy with what you buy or where you go or what you are doing. Security has to do with a feeling, not anything tangible. We've had only one car for the last four years, but recently bought a car for me. It was not so much I wanted a car, but I wanted the freedom and independence it would bring me.

Does money bring happiness? There are tales of lottery winners who are unhappy for a multitude of reasons. One big drawback is often relatives and others who want a gift of money or want a loan. If money is your sole goal in life, there is a major drawback. No matter how much you have, you may feel there is never enough.

3. Other People

This is the most misunderstood of what you can't count on, and what can bring the most unhappiness. We often ask too much of others — to love us, to do what we want, to do what we expect, to not let us down, to not die. It's all about what we think and want from others, not what's best for them.

Our bodies are in a constant decay. We're not meant to last forever. People will leave you. They will physically die. As we get older, cells become weary. We aren't as able to run, walk, remember as easily as when we were younger. We weren't meant to last forever. If we accept this, we will be able to age with gracefulness and not regret, even when we turn 30, 40 . . . .

What is a positive role regarding others? You know problems arise when you expect something from someone and they don't follow through. If you chose your role to be giving to people vs. expecting something from them, life can be more meaningful and positive for you and them.

In the words of Roy T. Bennett, *The Light in the Heart*, "Most of us must learn to love people and use things rather than loving things and using people."

If you can't count on anything physical, wealth, people to love and support you, is there anything you can count on?

What You Can Count On

There is hope. One of the main reasons I'm writing this book is to share with you what you can count on.

1. Intuition

The most important thing is to look inside yourself. Welcome your intuition, your gateway to your inner wisdom.

One of the main reasons Pinocchio had trouble with his journey was he never listened to Jiminy Cricket, his conscience and higher self, who was constantly trying to help him. Trust your inklings of Jiminy Cricket. They will serve you well. Sometimes your body will give you a hint if something is true and right for you. Some people get goose bumps on their arms when something rings true to them. Or you may have another indication. Watch for it. Probably you already do.

2. Own Experiences

Even though you have filters you look through (your unresolved experiences), let your own experiences be your guide instead of someone else's. If you understand we all have filters and most people only have opinions about what they consider facts, it is easier to be open to what others have to say. There may be some truth there, enabling us to learn from news sources and other people rather than being defensive. As you live, you can clean your filters by learning from your experiences rather than engaging in negativity about them.

3. Universal Principles

In my late 20s, I started on a lifelong search to find what I could count on. Many religions said they were right and others were wrong. Who knew the truth? Most people did not speak the truth but had only opinions about it, and I had yet to discover how to tell what was really true for me. Even science was changing as more and more was discovered.

When I was that age, there were no computers, no Google, no Siri, no Alexa. There were books however and I discovered two books with interviews with people who had near-death experiences. (There are many more today.[1]) People came back and told what they had experienced on the "other side." All were asked if they had learned to love. In addition, one was asked if he knew the Universal Principles. I had never heard of those before, so I decided, since it seemed to be that important, I would spend the rest of my life searching for them. Perhaps they were what I had been looking for, what I could put my trust in.

Over the last 55 years, I have found them in spirituality and psychology. The full list of over 30 principles is found in my life work, *Finding the Lost UNIVERSAL PRINCIPLES. The Three Little Pigs unlock the door*. In that book, I condensed the principles into a few. After reading my book, a friend said he had teenagers and they really needed to know "this stuff." And so, I started to write this book for you.

In these next couple of chapters, you will find truths that you can judge to be true or not according to your own experience. The universal principles are the main reason I started writing this book. They have been true and invaluable to me, and perhaps will be for you.

How has the issue of trust been important to you?

_____

_____

_____

[1] Some books on near-death experiences: *Imagine Heaven* by John Burke, Baker Books, Publisher; *Life After Life* by Raymond Moody, HarperCollins Publisher; *Proof of Heaven*, Eben Alexander, Simon & Schuster Publisher; *To Heaven and Back*, Mary C. Neal, WaterBrook Publisher.

NOTES

THE "HOW TO BE HAPPY AND PEACEFUL" TEST

In the Pinocchio story, he didn't have to take this happy and peaceful test in school, because he didn't go to school. Yet, he was still taking the test of living, of being happy and peaceful. For Pinocchio it held the answers for being "brave, truthful, and unselfish."

You are taking this test now. Was this test sprung on you by surprise and you didn't have a chance to study for it? What text were you supposed to study beforehand?

Relax. You can take as long as you want to take this test and you can go back and change the answers you made previously. You won't find the text you need to study for this test at school, in a bookstore, or on Amazon, but here it is for you. The text is called *The Universal Principles Book for Life*, giving you the answers for a happy and peaceful life. You need to be aware of these principles. Then, it's up to you to test them out for yourself as you live. Neale Donald Walsch explains,". . . words may help you understand something, but experience allows you to know."

You may have thought you had the right book to study before now.

> I'd always believed that a life of quality, enjoyment, and wisdom was my human birthright . . . I never suspected that I would have to learn how to live . . . ways of seeing the world I had to master before I could awaken to a simple, happy, uncomplicated life.
> —Dan Millman , *The Life You Were Born To Live*.

The common book most people use for this test, probably the one your parents used, told you to trust what you can see (including the health of your own physical body); to have enough money to live well; and to be with other people you like, like you, and support you. The reason that book doesn't prepare you for this important test is because that subject matter is always changing. The physical is always decaying into other forms, there never seems to be enough money, and other people may never live up to your expectations. The text on Universal Principles lists the correct subject matter to get the right answers for the test.

You have an advantage over Pinocchio because he never had that book, but now you do. Here it is, in this next chapter, (which is actually a book within this book,) *The Universal Principles Book for Life.*

NOTES

THE UNIVERSAL PRINCIPLES BOOK FOR LIFE

Pinocchio never had this textbook. He didn't go to school, but you don't get this book at school, anyway. Without schooling, his reading ability may have been a challenge, but you are fortunate, you can read and understand.

This book covers seven principles.

#1: All is One

Everything is one — all people, all religions, and time and space.

#2: The Balance of Life

What may seem like opposites tend to balance each other, an affirmation of the wholeness and oneness of life.

#3: The Unseen Controls the Seen

What is unseen, on the inner (feelings, thoughts) controls the outer, the seen (what we do and what we have).

#4: Cause and Effect Always Occur Together

One always follows another, as if in a spiral.

#5: Change is a Constant

Change is. Make it your friend.

#6: We Are Spiritual Beings

That knowledge is our deepest essence and desire.

#7: It's All About Energy and Vibration

Science knew it all along. All is energy and is in different levels of vibration. Nothing is ever lost, but just changes form.

Principle #1: All is One

If the only concept you retain from reading this textbook on principles is All is One, it would have been worth your read.

Correct grammar would say All are One, however, in this case, all is singular. 1 + 1 = 1.

As humans, we are starting to understand that everything is one. Father Thomas P. Bonacci, Executive Director of the Interfaith Peace Project, says we are beginning to understand that all is "interrelated, interconnected, and interdependent."

The concept of oneness is so important that if we would put it into practice, it alone could be the solution to all the problems of the world. Many of our laws protecting what we hold dear would not be needed. If we knew our earth and solar system were one, we would have true respect and stewardship of the land and its animals, and the concept of climate change would be more widely understood, accepted, and relevant laws enacted. If we knew that as a people we were one, there would be compassion for our fellow human beings — no hunger, no pillage, and no wars. If we knew that time and space were one, our lives would be much richer, living in the present and not bound by the future (fear and worry) or the past (regret, blame, guilt, or resentment). If we knew that all religions were one, we'd no longer be judgmental, close-minded or competitive. We would focus on the essence of each and work together with no divisiveness.

James Cameron, director of *Avatar*, stated:

> *Avatar* asks us to see that everything is connected, all human beings to each other, and we to the Earth. And if you have to go four and a half light-years to another made-up planet to appreciate this miracle of the world we have right here, well, you know what, that's the wonder of cinema right there, that's the magic...

Neale Donald Walsch thoughts on oneness:

> Everything would change. Everything. Politics would change, economics would change, relationships would change, your ideas, about careers and parenting and sexuality and conflict resolution and the purpose of all Life — everything — would change.

All Physical is One

This concept is a scientific truth that has been accepted in principle for decades. Everything is energy and vibration; it never goes away, it just changes form. The Earth's oneness was not a clear concept with the general public until the astronauts went out and took pictures, looking back at Earth. We then saw the reality of what our physical universe has always been. The Earth is one living organism.

Naturalists and ecologists know that when one animal goes extinct, it affects the whole planet. If that animal or insect goes extinct, its predator could also die, as will its predator, setting off a chain reaction. This is why laws are protecting even the most "insignificant" living creature that is limited in number, be it the spotted owl, the red-legged frog or the checker spotted butterfly. Projects have been stopped or redesigned because of endangered species and their habitats. There is nothing in the physical realm that has a separate relationship from anything else.

The water cycle, an excellent example of a closed physical system, is so elementary that you were probably taught it in school. That is why environmentalists are so concerned about polluting our water, a closed system. In fun, I often like to ask people if they know Cleopatra or Napoleon may have once drunk the water they are drinking right now.

Masaru Emoto's book, *The Hidden Messages in Water*, gives an unusual insight into physical relationships. Mr. Emoto's studies on water show that water responds to vibrations from the written word. Words send off a unique vibration that water senses. When one writes words on a piece of paper and wraps that around a bottle of water, the water reacts to the words. (He shows this by the crystals the water forms after reading the vibrations from the words.) Water exposed to "Thank you" formed beautiful hexagonal crystals, but water exposed to the word "Fool" produced crystals similar to the water exposed to heavy-metal music, malformed and fragmented. Mr. Emoto's research applies to all of us. Our body is 70% water. We all have a choice about what words we use and it can make a difference with how our body will function.

The fact "all physical is one" may seem innocuous when it doesn't affect you personally. As young people, you are becoming well aware if we don't handle our climate change challenges right now, our earth might become inhabitable for you. That is personal.

How do you see everything physical as one?

_____

_____

_____

_____

_____

_____

_____

_____

All People Are One

Before we talk about other people, we must look at the most important person — our self. What would it mean to be at one with one's self? At one with what?

We have a higher self that knows what it means to be a genuine human being, our birthright. This is before the layers of negativity have clouded us. It's our Jiminy Cricket, our still small voice, from the Pinocchio story.

Our reactions to things that have happened in our past keep us believing and claiming our lack of self-oneness. We can uncover and heal these wounds through the use of psychologists, psychiatrists, psychics, and even all by ourselves. It has to do with decisions we make, and we make a lot of them.

We see many needs in the world and wish for a change. That certainly has not happened with the military or legislative bodies. Change can only be lasting if it starts at the smallest unit, inside you and me. It's bringing about the oneness in ourselves that enables the right decisions and therefore, right action. As a person, we have a great deal of power over ourselves, more than we realize. I'm reminded of the song, "Man in the Mirror," sung by Michael Jackson.

> I'm Starting With The Man In The Mirror
> I'm Asking Him To Change His Ways
> And No Message Could Have Been Any Clearer
> If You Wanna Make The World A Better Place
> (If You Wanna Make The World A Better Place)
> Take a Look at Yourself,
> And Then Make A Change . . .

Oneness with others may be somewhat tougher to accept than the oneness with the physical universe or even oneness with ourselves. How could I be one with someone who is so different in background and thinking, or so difficult to be around? As we come to understand ourselves, it is possible to feel more at ease with others.

Oneness is less evident when one only looks at the outer. It's on the inner where we see the similarity. We all desire to be loved, acknowledged, and accepted. We desire to be at one with the higher being that we are, thereby living in inner peace and thankfulness. Look deeply into yourself and others to see your oneness with them. I like to think we are all in camouflage, different on the outside, but the same on the inside. We are all in disguise. Every day is Halloween.

I've been a theatre actress for over 30 years. Acting has taught me to be a more compassionate person. With each different role I've played, I had to dig inside myself to find those attitudes, emotions, and ideas of that person. When I was able to find and accept these attributes inside myself, I could become that character. That led me to accept people like that in real life. I now know I am everything, but choose to show certain parts of myself with which I want to identify and want others to see.

The Ho'noponopono Hawaii healing system that is used by Dr. Ihaleakala Hew Len of Hawaii is a profound example of the principle of oneness. Joe Vitale's book, *zero limits*, details how Dr. Len cured a complete ward of mentally ill patients without ever seeing them. He read each chart and then meditated as recited, "I love you. I'm sorry. Please forgive me. Thank you." The prayer was directed to God with intent and knowledge that the same illness that was in the mentally ill patient, was also in himself. He was asking God to forgive the cause in himself. No one knows exactly how this "miracle" happened, but the whole ward was healed by Dr. Len's actions.

The masters of the ages have said self-knowledge is the most important knowledge you can possess. Self-knowledge leads you to the truth of oneness and compassion for your fellow man.

Neal Donald Walsch states:

You must first see your Self as worthy before you can see another as worthy. You must first see your Self as blessed before you can see another as blessed. You must first know your Self to be holy before you can acknowledge holiness in another.

Rumi (Ramana Maharshi), a 13th-century Persian poet, Islamic scholar, theologian, and Sufi mystic, when asked how should we treat others, answered, "There are no others."

How do you experience oneness with others?

_____
_____
_____
_____
_____
_____
_____

All Religions Are One

Throughout the ages, many world conflicts were waged in the name of religion — the Inquisition, the Israeli wars, the Shiites and the Sunnis, Ireland, China, and Tibet. It's as old as Cain and Able and continues to this day. Rather than leading us to love our fellow man, religious dogma and intolerance have produced thoughts of superiority and inferiority, separation, fear, hatred, torture, and killing.

There is an Ojibwa Indian saying, "No tree has branches so foolish as to fight amongst themselves."

Bahá'u'lláh, of the Bahai faith, also uses the analogy of the tree. "The tabernacle of unity hath been raised; regard ye not one another as strangers. Ye are the fruits of one tree, and the leaves of one branch."

What has gone wrong? Humorously, this is the way it is.

NONSEQUITUR © 2007 Wiley Miller, Dist. By Andrews McMeel SYNDICATION, Reprinted with permission. All rights reserved

Mandalas show various religions, all with equal emphasis, not one doctrine being superior to another.

Unitarian Universalist

Creative Initiative Foundation, 1980s

Amara Wahaba Karuna. Karunaarts.com

Newlifeparadigm.com

Sai Baba, an Indian spiritual master revered by both Hindus and Muslims, said in 1968:

> I have come to light the lamp of Love in your hearts, to see that it shines day by day with added luster. I have not come on behalf of any exclusive religion. I have not come on a mission of publicity for a sect or creed or cause, nor have I come to collect followers for a doctrine. I have no plan to attract disciplines or devotees into my fold or any fold. I have come to tell you of this unitary faith, this spiritual principle, this path of Love, this virtue of Love, this duty of Love, this obligation of Love.

You may have seen this bumper sticker.

STAMPANDSHOUT.COM

Kryon of Magnetic Service, an entity who is channeled by various psychics, sees the acceptance of others and their paths in a non-judgmental way.

> Blessed are the human beings who search for Home in their own way, in a building of their own choice, with a priest of their choice, in any way that makes their heart feel the love of God in their way, for they will have light in their heart and have a better life for it.

In the Bible, John 14:2, Jesus is quoted: "In my Father's house are many mansions; if it were not so, I would have told you."

I envision each religion having a spoke on a wheel. A wagon wheel is a good image because the hub of the wheel is important.

In our basic understanding of our religion, we are on a spoke near the outside rim edge of the wheel. We see a great distance between our own spoke and those other spokes (religions) on each side of us. As our understanding becomes deeper in our own religion, and as we each move toward the center on our own spoke, the distances are closer to the spokes on each side and we see more similarities. When we get to the center of the wheel, the hub, we see all spokes end up in the same place. All religions are saying the same thing. It is Oneness with God/the All.

Neale Donald Walsch in *Conversations with God* calls this remembering:

> There is no doctrine in the center, no rules, no place to come to or report to. You don't have to join anything because you already have. You are a piece of God, in the family of spirit. You communicate directly with God. It is the place of Oneness.

If we are militant about our beliefs, thinking it is the only way, and are judgmental about another's, that indicates we have not entered into a deeper understanding and the true essence of our own religion. Father Tomas P. Bonacci, Executive Director of the Interfaith Peace Project has said if people have trouble with the interfaith concept, it's their own religion they have a problem with.

"Sai Inspires" calls the peacefulness of the hub, Bliss:

> Truly speaking, it is not difficult to know what the basis of life is, and what should be the goal of life. Bliss should be the goal, and one must seek it in all earnestness. The human body is temporary; the pleasure that it can give also is fleeting. Therefore, one must seek that which is permanent, that is to say, God, or what is the same thing. Bliss. It is meaningless to seek this Bliss by way of instruments that are impermanent. The body can give only bodily pleasure, and the mind can at best give only mental satisfaction. But these do not represent Bliss.

The hub is rich because each religion gives jewels to it in the form of principles. There are a thousand different religions on the Earth, but some of the predominant ones, are as follows:

The Bahá'í faith focuses on the principle of oneness — one God, one human race, and the different religions being evolutions of God's will and purpose for humanity. Followers believe the time has come for all peoples to unite into a peaceful and integrated society.

Buddhism's Eight-Fold Path symbolizes right views, aims, speech, conduct, living, effort, mindfulness, and meditation. When followed with sincerity and discipline, these paths lead to enlightenment.

Christianity believes God loves all. It points to the underlying oneness and interrelationship of all people.

    1) Loving thy neighbor as thyself.
    2) The Golden Rule of doing unto others as you would have them do unto you.
    3) Judge not, lest you be judged.

Confucianism focuses on ethical teachings, the highest of which is the oneness of all people. — Jen: benevolence, humaneness towards others.

Gnosticism believes in the Oneness of all and provides a guide to help determine what is true, emphasizing that one must trust one's highest self/one's soul/God within, and asks us to focus on our own experience, not just believe someone else's.

In Hinduism, non-violence and respect for all life are practiced. They see all are a part of God.

Humanism celebrates the best in human attributes, leading to the spirit of enlightenment, which is to be used for the good of all.

The beliefs of Islam include getting to know one another, respecting one another, and upholding our collective human dignity. Sufism, the more mystical path of Islam, emphasizes the truth found in all religions.

Jainism emphasizes harmlessness to all and focuses on "Three Jewels:"

1) right faith (clear sight)
2) right knowledge (aka, Universal Principles and Spiritual Truths)
3) right conduct (action based on right faith and right knowledge)

In Judaism, a basic belief is all things were designed to have meaning and purpose, as part of a divine order of one creator of everything.

The Native American spirit reminds us all creatures are our brothers and sisters, and for us to honor the spirits and sacred energy in all life forms.

Sikhism's main teachings emphasize God-realization, the importance of having a teacher for guidance and instruction, and the importance of detachment from physical matters.

Shintoism morality is based on what is beneficial to the group and emphasizes right practice, sensibility, and attitude.

In Taoism, the Yin Yang symbolizes balance and harmony, a symbol of oneness, and suggests those who understand duality and choose to live beyond it, will have lives of wholeness and compassion.

The Unitarian Universalist philosophy embodies We Are One, welcoming all humankind, believing the diversity leads to beauty, strength, courage, and respect for the independence of all existence.

Wicca is earth-centered and emphasizes the importance of protecting the ecology and resources of our planet.

Zoroastrianism focuses on the dualities in life: truth and falsehood, and the "Destructive Principle" and the "Bounteous Principle."

No matter what religious doctrine we follow, if our being is not peaceful we have not understood and experienced the essence of our own religion. In the hub, all is one, because there is great understanding and compassion. With compassion, one sees beyond the outer, superficial things that seem to separate us. Living in the hub is true inner peace, the "peace of God that passeth all understanding." One understands the warning "Never criticize a man until you walk a mile in his moccasins." (Native American adage)

The universe urges us to live in the hub of the wheel, and to acknowledge the jewels of all religions. Much depth in beauty and richness reside there. The Law of Allowing from the Abraham-Hicks writings challenges us to welcome and learn from a variety of disciplines. They advise us to accept them all, which is to accept all of God and all of one's self. To deny any of them is to deny a part of God and one's self.

This Principle of Oneness is the key to "heaven on Earth" because it generates a feeling of love, overcoming separation. Most people wish for this outcome (whether they call it that or not), but it does not happen by wishing or by chance. In *The Journey Home, a Kryon Parable (The Story of Michael Thomas and the Seven Angels)* channeled by Lee Carroll, the process is detailed for how one can experience heaven without dying because heaven on earth is a state of being, not a place. A key to heaven or hell for our world and ourselves is to examine our beliefs to see what aligns with the Universal Principle of Oneness, and to see how we are working with it or against it.

How do you see the oneness of religions?

_____

_____

_____

_____

_____

Time and Space are One

Hold on. This may be out of your comfort zone. We are learning more and more from metaphysics and quantum physics about the dimensions of time and space. The old thinking of linear time, where it is understood only as a straight line of before and after, is being looked at again. We are now encouraged to consider time as interdimensional. It is revolutionary to think this way. With humor, the spell check in Word thinks the word interdimensional is wrong and keeps urging me to change it to "one-dimensional."

One way to understand "interdimensional" is, instead of viewing time as a straight line, see it as a building with three stories. Even this explanation is linear; interdimensional would be stacked but similar to a helix, all intertwining, and mixing. All are in the now, where the past, present, and future are all one.

Here is a diagram approximating the difference between linear time and quantum time.

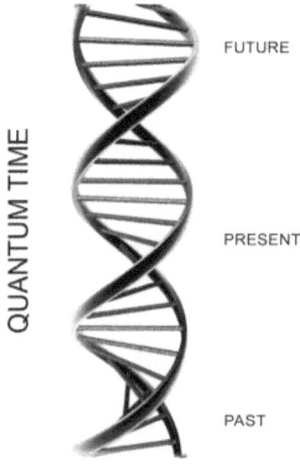

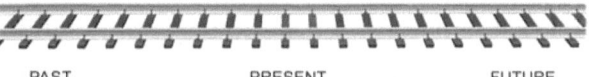

About 10 years ago, I tested the concept that past, present, and future were stacked on each other. Could I really access the past? I did. I cured myself of a disease called fibromyalgia I'd had for over 15 years. The process I used is called Quantum Healing learned from Kryon of Magnetic Service, an entity that can be accessed in meditation by some. He said because time is stacked and not linear, we could take ourselves back in time before we had the disease. First of all, I handled the disease psychologically. I thought about and gave up any benefit I was getting from the disease ... sympathy and being less responsible at home and in the community. Then I concentrated on taking myself back in time. Within a few minutes, I could move my joints with no pain. I could sit with no pain. I was amazed. People have asked me how I did that and I said it took belief and focus.

Another application: wishing for something one doesn't have now, but hoping for in the future, is an error in interdimensional terms. In a new way, seeing that one already has what one desires is more accurate because the past, present, and future are one. Some who have approached their desires as already accomplished have found this to be true. I would encourage you to experiment with this concept yourself. The Universe may seem to work in strange ways according to our limited thinking.

The movie, *What the Bleep Do We Know!?*, states, "If you can't believe it, you won't see it." I have experienced that many times. When I was pregnant with my first child, I'd look around and it seemed as though every woman was pregnant. I just had not noticed the pregnant women before. Many times after learning something new, I'd see it again and again in different contexts. Or when I'd meet someone new, soon after I'd consistently run into them again. It shows how important our consciousness is. Dr. Wayne Dwyer stated, "When you change the way you look at things, the things you look at change."

Oneness gives us insight into phobias. If not traceable to an experience in one's current lifetime, the instance possibly was stored (cell memory) from a previous one and then activated by the current one. Often the phobia may not be seen until the age when that experience occurred in a previous life. Sometimes the knowledge alone of the true origin can heal the phobia/fear.

Some say birthmarks are evidences of traumas from a past life. I have an acquaintance who has a round birthmark near his spine on this back. Indeed, sometimes he acts as if he were stabbed in the back.

Kryon of Magnetic Service has said those who are autistic have problems because they are not linear thinkers in our linear world. What if interdimensionally they are at a higher level, and we, the linear, are the challenged ones?

The oneness of time and space, and human beings beginning to think interdimensionally, are foreign to our linear trained mind, against almost everything we have been taught in school. As you think about physically traveling to new places, you might want to play with psychic travel (as we do in our dreams).

How do the past, present, and future play out as one for you?

_____

_____

_____

_____

_____

_____

_____

Principle #2: The Balance of Life

The Yin Yang is a common symbol. You've probably seen it before. The symbol comes from the Taoist (pronounced Daoist) tradition. But what does it mean? It makes sense that it follows Principle #1, Oneness, because it's a visual symbol of oneness. This symbol however shows oneness is more complex.

The Yin (dark) is the passive, negative, receptive, water, emotional, a female source. The Yang (light) is the active, positive, fire, mental, a male source. The S-like curve symbolizes the dance of these energies; nothing is absolute in itself but changing, fluid and active. Even in the dark side, there is a hint of white, and the white has a hint of dark, showing the complexity and inter-relationships between the two.

Why is this symbol important? Just as with Principle #1, you can trust this concept to be trustworthy and help you with your life.

My first experience with the opposites of the Yin Yang was to understand every person has both a feminine principle of a passive, expansive, receptive, emotional side and a masculine principle of active, fixed, focused, mental side. Generally, we have strength in one or the other. We may call it being an extrovert (male principle) or an introvert (female principle). We are born whole, but as a child, we decided to develop a certain way to get love and attention from our parents. We don't have to carry those stereotypes with us our whole life. We're whole and our challenge is to develop our undeveloped side so we have both sides to respond creatively to what happens to us.

In my 30s, I had a recurring dream where I was running around my house, panicked, locking doors and windows just before two "robbers" reached them. Knowing dreams are our subconscious trying to help us (especially with recurring dreams), I followed the advice of a friend who said to let the "robbers" in. It took courage to do this, but when I did, I found these were not robbers but "friends" — my husband and young son. They said they were there to help me. I knew the masculine principle was my challenge to develop, and they were symbols of the mature masculine and the immature masculine there to help. As soon as I understood this, I never had the dream again.

I find it amusing when people refer to my husband as my other half. With a smile, I gently respond to them, "We are both whole." We are drawn to those who have the qualities we lack, and most often the persons we choose to be our friends and our significant other have strengths in the half we are missing. The term "he completes me" is also showing that the other person has the strength that we need.

However, our challenge is to be grateful and learn from the other person so we can be whole, not dependent, and not irritated when the other person does not respond in life like we would. By learning from them, we are reclaiming our wholeness and our freedom.

Corrie Ten Boom, concerning her personal experience in a Nazi concentration camp, recorded another example of the Yin Yang at work in *The Hiding Place*. She was interned in a barracks that was infested with fleas, and all the women were bitten. (This situation with fleas seems especially negative to me since I have an allergic reaction to fleas and dislike the bites so much.) While there, the women wanted to discuss religion and the Bible, which was strictly forbidden.

Despite the flea irritation, Ms. Ten Boom accepted the flea situation. She had the faith that fleas were not all negative; there was a positive side, even though she was not sure what it was. Later she found out the reason they were able to have secret religious discussions was that the guards stayed away from her barracks because the fleas were so bad there. That was a positive to the negative of the fleas.

Three pairs of powerful dualities many people find confusing are good and evil, right and wrong, positive and negative. I, too, wondered why some people thought something was good and right, while others thought the same thing was evil and wrong. Who is right? Does this mean good and evil are not objective, not absolute, and not black and white? Absolutely. Good and evil are subjective judgments, up to the person's own value system and beliefs as to how to label something. It's decided by one's own value judgments, and what one believes is true.

William Shakespeare counsels, "... there is nothing either good or bad but thinking makes it so..."

Therefore, this Christmas gift bag makes an appropriate request of Santa:

© Hallmark Licensing

If duality exists, is there something only good with no evil, or only evil without a hint of good? No. The universal principle of the Yin Yang says there are always the two — see the small dots in the opposite sides. Not just black or just white; not just evil or just good.

The New Earth, by Eckhart Tolle, presents a story of a man who understood duality and therefore did not judge something as good or evil. He aligned himself with a higher order. This is the story.

> ... of a wise man who won an expensive car in a lottery. His family and friends were very happy for him and came to celebrate. "Isn't it great!" they

said. "You are so lucky." The man smiled and said, "Maybe." For a few weeks, he enjoyed driving the car. Then one day a drunken driver crashed into his new car at an intersection and he ended up in the hospital, with multiple injuries. His family and friends came to see him and said, "That was really unfortunate." Again the man smiled and said, "Maybe." While he was still in the hospital, one night there was a landslide and his house fell into the sea. Again his friends came the next day and said, "Weren't you lucky to have been here in (the) hospital." Again he said, "Maybe."

Be careful what you wish for; you might get it. Have you seen the downside of your desire? I have fond memories of the TV program *Fantasy Island,* which ran from 1978-1984 because it was such a good example of duality. There were stories of visitors to a unique resort island, which could fulfill any fantasy requested. These adventures should be impossible, but this island could accommodate them — visits to any time they wanted, meet absolutely anyone they wanted, enact any feat they wanted. The program always showed the people having to face the negative aspect of their dream.

In one episode, a man wished to be irresistible to all women. He was given a special cologne, but he used too much of it. He found that it was not as positive as he had imagined, having women chase him all the time, and he decided the only woman he really wanted was his fiancée. In another, "Bet A Million," a couple travels to Fantasy Island dreaming of meeting a wealthy investor. They weren't aware that the meeting would be at the Baccarat table with all their assets on the line. They had to risk it all to make their dream come true.

Being judgmental is the cause of wars, nationally and personally — the other is wrong and I am right. What does "In God We Trust" mean on our currency? What do we trust God to do? Do we trust Him and Her to be on our side, because we are always right, and the other country is always wrong? Is what is good for us, always good for them? Is that our collective thinking? If so, no wonder we go to war.

Why is an understanding of the duality of oneness important in daily life? In both positive and negative cases, it gives you a larger perspective of what is true and real. When something positive happens, it helps to be grounded and not be surprised when the drawback shows up. When something negative happens, it helps to resolve the negative: look for the positive, see the wholeness, and be free of the negative. There are common sayings in our culture about the opposites. "When one door closes, another one opens."

"Every cloud has a silver lining." It helps one to resolve all that is considered negative and to live in the positive.

When our son was in high school, he told me for my 40th birthday he was going to give me eternal life. I chuckled and said I wasn't sure I wanted that. Then, he told me to tell him what I thought was the most important thing in life and he would pass it on to his children. It took me two years to write him that letter about the balance of life (the Yin Yang) and how it applies to living. At that time, I did not understand the importance of Principle #1, All is One, or I may have included that as well.

Can you give an example of the Yin Yang balance in your life?

_____

_____

_____

_____

_____

_____

_____

_____

_____

_____

Principle #3: The Unseen Controls the Seen

Are you aware that the unseen controls you? This has nothing to do with science fiction and has everything to do with psychology.

The unseen are non-physical; they cannot be seen with our physical senses of sight or touch. They are energies — feelings, emotions, ideas, beliefs, concepts, principles, and attitudes. The seen are what we see in the physical world around us — people, houses, cars, furniture, trees, and mountains.

The seen is easy to accept because it is visible. The unseen is elusive because it requires more attention, a higher level of consciousness. "Some of the most beautiful things in life cannot be seen or touched — they are felt with the Heart." (Helen Keller, on a plaque by L. Voskuil-Dutter)

I first got a glimpse of the unseen, the deeper part of myself, when I was at a seminar in the 1990s. Participants did an exercise in pairs in which the other person asked you over and over, "Who are you?" I quickly went through all my titles and roles and then . . . I went into another kind of dimension. I became some kind of pure awareness. I moved to just outside Earth, encircled it and embraced it as though I was only consciousness. That is what I called it at the time. I was truly euphoric and remained in that state for about a week. I didn't know what happened to me, but now I consider it my first actual experience of my soul, my true and deepest self. I have had other experiences of my true self recently, most of the time through meditation. Words cannot explain the magnificence of them.

One of the most important issues females have is to accept their own bodies. Outer standards seem to be set for us and we compare ourselves with others. Indeed, psychologists agree that the outer manifestations of being overweight must be changed from the inner unseen. One cannot only fix the outer seen. This issue has deep-seated psychological causes. Why do we feel we have to eat to comfort ourselves? Comfort ourselves because of what? What need is being covered up? What is really missing in our lives?

You are still young, but watch out for identifying with the physical and using that as a symbol of success. I chuckled when I was behind a "sexy," new Lexus sports car whose license plate read CMYCAR. Did he identify with his car or not? Is he more than his car? Are those who have a car like his better than those who don't? If someone doesn't have it and someone else does, they fight to get it. It's one of the causes of war. If the issue of the car doesn't strike you, think oil.

Neale Donald Walsh has told us the correct flow is Being, then Doing, then Having. If our Being is healthy, then what you Do will be of no harm to yourself or others, and you will be happy with what you Have. Our society has the flow backwards and thinks you have to Have something, to be able to Do something, and then you will Be happy. They have the flow backward, and correctly it is from the unseen to the seen and not the seen to the unseen.

It is crucial that our Doing/Action is coming from a place of correct Being/A Win for all. As a nation, we need to make some important decisions soon about our environment. What we Do with the environment will mean a planet you will Have that will be inhabitable or not for you, your children and grandchildren. What we Do about addressing police brutality will allow people to live in peace or with fear.

In the Bible, Matthew 19:24 states, "It is easier for a camel to go through the eye of a needle, than for a rich man to enter into the kingdom of God." Scholars disagree on the origin of this saying, however, the common understanding is you have to unload your camel to get through the narrow gates of the cities. This does not mean you have to give away your worldly possessions. Symbolically this means we have to unload ourselves from the beliefs we think we need to have to live in inner peace, like having the wrong plants in our garden. The verse pertains to the unseen beliefs and not the seen physical possessions. We are not anything like what others see on our outside — our possessions, our job titles. Our treasure is within, the unseen.

I entered a major depression in my early 50s because I felt I was a nobody. I now refer to this as my desert period. Many of my friends had advanced degrees, "valued" professions, titles, and status. I did not consider myself "successful." I was not a medical doctor, a lawyer, an architect, or some other highly valued title. I allowed myself to be brainwashed that the job title was what made a person of value. I was depressed, thinking that the outer role was what was important in life. I was a college graduate and a licensed Clinical Laboratory Scientist, but stopped working when the family came along. I told my medical doctor about feeling depressed and not having meaning in my life because I was not a high-level professional. She said it certainly didn't come from being a medical doctor. That shocked me.

This doesn't mean it's not important to have a profession, but it won't necessarily bring you happiness and the sense of security that you deeply desire.

> We must ask ourselves: What am I NOT? I'm not my house, not my car, not my relationships. We are NO THING. Once we realize this, it will then be pretty easy to go through the eye of a needle.
> —Dr. Carl J. Calleman and Mr. Ian Lungold

Many things people interpret as outer and seen, really have to do with the inner and unseen. With the Age of Aquarius, the hippie generation took off their clothes, but the Age was about the unseen, not the seen. The Age was calling for a bare mind, an open mind, not a bare physical body. When alchemists were trying to turn lead into gold, they were mistaken, thinking that was a physical formula. Instead the formula was psychological. They wanted to turn lead (soft and not pure), into silver (soft and pure), and finally into gold (hard and pure). A psychological movement was being revealed — from untruth to truth, from unconsciousness to consciousness. It had nothing to do with the physical metal, but what it symbolized.

Outer experiences are captivating, and people love the heightened emotions they gain from mountain climbing, deep-sea diving, hang gliding, bungee jumping, ballooning and the like. Those of us who were old enough to remember were captivated with Apollo 11 when Neil Armstrong set his foot on the moon, July 16, 1969. However, the experience of inner space (the unseen) brings the greatest high. The evolution of our species has to do with the exploration of the unseen, our inner space.

The unseen controls events. Have you wondered why things happen the way they do? Why does a person act that way? Why do some people get all the "luck?" *The Journey Home* by Lee Carroll, taken from the knowledge of Kryon, states, "Things are not as they may seem." The unseen is at work. What if everything that happens is part of a larger plan of which we are not aware in our limited consciousness? I am fond of the terms Divine Chaos and Divine Timing, both involving the unseen. Divine Chaos is especially interesting because it contains a duality. Our Higher Self/The All considers all things Divine, while our egos may call them Chaos. Levels of consciousness make the difference. Things appear chaotic because we don't see far enough. Some call Divine Chaos, Divine Right Action.

One day, I had an experience at the bank. The ATM wasn't working so I had to come back later. I was not pleased. When I came back to make my deposit, the woman before me had left her ATM card in the machine. I grabbed it and ran after her. It made me wonder. Was the reason I wasn't able to use the ATM before was so the timing would be right to help that woman? If this synchronicity didn't happen, how would it have changed her day, her health, and her family? My day, my health, my family. The whole scenario was Divine Timing In Action.

What if all the experiences that cause us "difficulty" are for the good of ourselves or others — avoiding a car accident, helping another, meeting or not meeting someone. The bank ATM is a simple example, but what I learned was when things don't go my way, it could be Divine Chaos and Divine Timing at work, and a positive occurrence. If remembered, this concept could help one stay positive in light of a potential negative. "Things are not as they may seem."

Kryon of Magnetic Service, states 3D screams (the physical, the seen, the obvious, the linear), and spirit whispers (the emotional, the spiritual, the elusive, the unseen, the interdimensional). A profound change in consciousness occurs when one wants to become aware of the whispers of the unseen. Maybe you were born on that path. For others, it may take some kind of exaggerated experience to cause the occurrence.

We don't understand what we really are because we focus on the seen. We need to be in touch with the unseen, where the power is. Marianne Williamson in *A Return To Love: Reflections on the Principles of A Course in Miracles* states:

> Our deepest fear is not that we are inadequate. Our deepest fear is that we are powerful beyond measure. It is our light, not our darkness that most frightens us. We ask ourselves, Who am I to be brilliant, gorgeous, talented, and fabulous? Actually, who are you not to be? You are a child of God. Your playing small does not serve the world. There is nothing enlightened about shrinking so that other people won't feel insecure around you. We were born to manifest the glory that is within us. And as we let our light shine, we unconsciously give other people permission to do the same. As we are liberated from our own fear, our presence automatically liberates others.

Happiness is an issue of the unseen. We all know the unseen is important or we would not be so interested in being happy. However, the road to finding happiness is misunderstood. Perhaps our forefathers did the country a disservice when they wrote in the Declaration of Independence that one of our rights was the "pursuit of happiness."

We search for happiness, but happiness can't be pursued directly, like a commodity. It doesn't matter what something is, you can be happy or not happy about it. Happiness is a decision, an attitude, a feeling. It should be enlightening (lighten your spirit) to know if you are unhappy, all you have to do is just change your attitude — perhaps see the positive side as a lesson learned, as the Yin Yang suggests. It's there.

I have been interested in having meaning in my life, not especially happiness. I, searched for meaning for a long time. I always thought it had something to do with what I was doing. Now, I realize everything has meaning. I discovered being is more important than doing, and being is what decides if something is meaningful. My being decided everything was meaningful, and it's the quality of mindfulness and presence with everything that gives meaning. I found meaning. Everything is filled with wonder and majesty. It is the sense we admire in children with their awe and wonder.

Ignorance of the unseen keeps us from understanding others and our world. It's not what we see that controls us, but what we don't see. We have inner-eye blindness. We often "jump to conclusions" in situations and communications with our spouse, our children, and others. If we are aware, our inner eyes can pick up feelings from others and ourselves that reveal information much more important than words alone.

The following story is from Dharma teachings.

A teacher teaching Maths (sic) to seven-year-old Arnav asked him, "If I give you one apple and one apple and one apple, how many apples will you have?" Within a few seconds, Arnav replied confidently, "Four..."

The dismayed teacher was expecting an effortless correct answer (three). She was disappointed. "Maybe the child did not listen properly," she thought. She repeated, "Arnav, listen carefully. If I give you one apple and one apple and one apple, how many apples will you have?"

Arnav had seen the disappointment on his teacher's face. He calculated again on his fingers. But within him, he was also searching for the answer that will make the teacher happy. His search for the answer was not for the correct one, but the one that will make his teacher happy. This time hesitatingly he replied, "Four..."

The disappointment stayed on the teacher's face. She remembered that Arnav liked strawberries. She thought maybe he doesn't like apples and that is making him lose focus. This time with an exaggerated excitement and twinkling in her eyes she asked, "If I give you one strawberry and one strawberry and one strawberry, then how many you will have?"

Seeing the teacher happy, young Arnav calculated on his fingers again. There was no pressure on him, but a little on the teacher. She wanted her new approach to succeed. With a hesitating smile, young Arnav enquired, "Three?

The teacher now had a victorious smile. Her approach had succeeded. She wanted to congratulate herself. But one last thing remained. Once again she asked him, "Now if I give you one apple and one apple and one more apple how many will you have?" Promptly Arnav answered, "Four!"

The teacher was aghast. "How Arnav, how?" she demanded in a little stern and irritated voice. In a voice that was low and hesitating, young Arnav replied, "Because I already have one apple in my bag."

During conversations with others, let's take some time to think about the apples that may be hidden.

In Robert Kiyosaki's book, *Rich Dad, Poor Dad*, there is an example of a child who is asked what is 2 + 2. Is the answer always 4? Not necessarily. It depends if you are in base 10 or 12. When someone gives you an answer that is different from what you expect, try to suspend your judgment. There might be an angle you have not considered. You must listen and understand with an open mind and an inner eye, for the unseen is at work.

Spiritualists and philosophers have said that until we start doing math in base 12 instead of base 10, we'll not be able to understand the true nature of our DNA and understand the full potential of the beings we really are.

As a stage actress, I learned that the unseen is in control. The audience comes to hear the subtext, not just the text. The feeling behind the words is what gives the interest and the flavor to the script. There is a world of difference in a delivery that is full of color and one done in a monotone.

I have no idea where the saying came from, "What you don't know won't hurt you." It is so untrue. The unseen is vital. I experienced a glaring example of this right before I retired. I was head of staff at a university department and one of the employees under my supervision stole from the department. The amount of money was minor, but it hurt the department because we had to go through an audit. It also hurt me, because I didn't catch it right away. What you don't know can hurt you because the unseen is as important as the seen.

The legal system has it right. Ignorance of the law is no excuse. The law still holds, and you are subject to it. That is why it is important to be aware of the unseen universal principles. They are the text of life and they always apply. If you don't obey, you will pay a price. If it is an outer law, you may pay a fine or go to jail. If it's an inner law, "inner jail" results — stress and dis-ease. Remember to row your boat gently, downstream. If that is not happening, there is a principle or truth you are probably fighting. Look for the unseen.

In his book, *The Power of Infinite Love and Gratitude*, Dr. Darren Weissman states: "All dis-ease (disease) comes from the inside out, from repressed negative feelings." The repressed emotion causes undue attention to it, resulting in stress. Even in Western medicine, it is accepted that stress makes any kind of unhealthy condition worse. A study in the *Journal of Advancement in Medicine* (Summer 1995) found that anger suppressed the immune system for five hours afterwards, and as the anger healed there was an increase of immunity for five to six hours.

If one is aware of unseen resistances (anger, fear, hurt, non-acceptance), one can resolve it. In doing so, it is possible to live with relatively little stress, boosting one's immune system. A possible outcome can be curing a disease. There are many reported cases of this nature.

Feelings and emotions have the power to control thoughts and actions. If you are angry, the outcome will be different than if you are accepting. The common saying is, "What goes around comes around." In the Bible (Galatians 6:7), Jesus said, "... Whatsoever a man soweth, that shall he also reap." If one sows corn, one gets corn, not wheat. If one sows positive, positive will be returned. If one sows negative, negative will be returned. It follows to never support a group that is ANTI anything. We are like magnets. It draws the negative. Think again. Instead of being anti-war, be pro-peace.

The principle has also been called the power of positive thinking, and many books have been written, including *The Power of Positive Thinking* by Norman Vincent Peale and *Think and Grow Rich* by Napoleon Hill. This law is reliable as gravity. Most of this is unseen and unconscious. We are not aware of what we are drawing to ourselves., which is as simple as telling a child not to do something. What do they do? Exactly what you told them not to do. The psyche doesn't understand the words no, not, and don't. I catch myself when I am playing golf, saying to myself, "I don't want to hit into the trees," and then I do. Or I think hitting to an uphill green is hard for me, and then it is. I am replacing these habitual thoughts with ones like, "I want the ball to go right there" and "I can do this." Being aware of all the negative talk on the fairways, it is surprising to me that some people play as well as they do.

I also got a chuckle out of the "Easy Button" from Staples, the office supply store. When you press it, it says, "That was easy." I gave one to our son at Christmas one year, telling him it was one of the secrets to life. He told me recently that he uses it all the time at work (a fast-paced, high stress lawyers' office).

Negative emotions (the unseen) are indicators we are drawing negativity to ourselves and giving it power. The emotions of hate, fear, greed, jealousy, blame, and judgment are profound feelings all of us are here to deal with in our lifetime. By mistake, we think by being angry or blaming that we are hurting the other person in some way. In reality, we are hurting ourselves and not them because they are in control of their own feelings. When we are aware we are feeling negative (even more powerful than thinking), we can stop and replace it with a feeling we want. This awareness, which is a lifelong challenge, helps us flow with the positive principles in life. As we gain higher levels of consciousness, we are more in control of our lives, negating a stressful and victim scenario. What we read and watch on our electronics is important. Filling our attention with people hurting other people takes a toll on us. We often become so used to it we don't realize the harm it creates. Many women of my generation still remember the shower scene in the original Hitchcock film, *Psycho*. (And they re-filmed it!) When you experience something, the experience never leaves you, it gets filed away somewhere in your brain.

When you want something and try hard to make it happen and it doesn't, you may want it consciously, but not subconsciously. You may be working against yourself, so your desire may not be forthcoming. What you think you want may not be the best for you in the long run, and your higher level of consciousness, like Jiminy, may be at work.

Then, too, the universe favors the positive. If your reason for wanting something comes from love (help for the family), it is more likely to be realized than if it comes from fear (afraid for the family). Some have found the best way to approach a desire is to see in gratitude that it is already accomplished. Michelangelo spoke of creating the Madonna and Child in the Sistine Chapel. As he was working on it, he saw it as already accomplished, and he was merely uncovering it. (This concept was mentioned earlier in the section on the oneness of time and space.)

The practice of meditation is the unseen in action. The power of being in the present moment vs. our thoughts raging about the past or the future can be a place of peace and harmony. It's the place of being "what is" vs. "what should or could be." It can be one of the keys to the peace that you may seek. Meditation is called a practice because it is just that — a practice in your quiet times for use in your other day-to-day activities. Some call it "heaven on earth."

This chapter about the unseen has been just words, but to live beyond the physical (seen) is a quality of those who are in various stages of enlightenment. The unseen has traditionally been the realm and expertise of the Masters such as Jesus, Mohammed, Buddha, and Lao Tzu. It is now spreading into the general population. An interest in the unseen has crept into our current and past television shows

— *The Good Place, Good Omen, God Friended Me, Joan of Arcadia, Touched by an Angel, The Secret,* and *Long Island Medium* to name a few.

The right kind of action needed on the planet comes from the unseen, an inner attitude of peace and love. Peace cannot be legislated or mandated. If we desire peace, we must look within and ask ourselves if we have a loving and peaceful nature. If the being is not right, the action won't be. One must rise above emotions and ideas that focus on the outer and those things that separate us. We must nurture the unseen. It is the new frontier that challenges us.

How does the unseen show up in your life?

_____
_____
_____
_____
_____
_____
_____
_____
_____
_____

Principle #4: Cause and Effect Always Occur Together

For every cause there is an effect, and for every effect there is a cause. On a personal level, one may find difficulty seeing cause and effect. How many of us believe we don't matter and our actions have no effect? We are just one individual and what impact do we make if we conserve energy, recycle our cans and bottles, and try to not use plastics (straws, containers, bags)? The effect may be so small or so far away we don't see it, but it still happens. Autopsies on animals have found some have ingested plastics blocking their digestive systems. Fish, whales, dolphins, and birds have died because of plastics wrapped around their flippers, beaks, wings, and feet.

What happens with all those electronics we responsibly recycle when they're outdated or don't work? The cause has an effect. They go away but don't go away. They're shipped overseas and dismantled in toxic waste dumps by people who themselves become toxic because of hazardous chemicals.

> The dirty little secret is that when you take [your electronic waste] to a recycler, instead of throwing it in a trashcan, about 80 percent of that material, very quickly, finds itself on a container ship going to a country like China, Nigeria, India, Vietnam, Pakistan — where very dirty things happen to it.
> — Jim Puckett, Basel Action Network executive director, reporting on National Public Radio

This doesn't mean we shouldn't use electronics, but just to know that the cause has an effect.

With our advances in communication, news spreads worldwide every second. The effect of that cause is newspaper companies, printing companies, and the postal service are having financial difficulties because their old methods are becoming obsolete.

Masaru Emoto, in *The Hidden Messages in Water*, gives an example of cause and effect, with the incidents occurring continents apart. He writes that he was conducting water experiments in Tokyo when he recorded an increased value in the level of vibrations of elements that are harmful to the human body. He redid his experiments, thinking he had somehow made a mistake. Not until the next day did he make a connection when he read in the newspaper about the invasion of Iraq, the onset of the first Gulf War. The weight of the bombs that were dropped on that first day of the war was equal to all the bombs dropped in Vietnam. Those vibrations were carried by water almost immediately from Iraq to Japan and the rest of the world.

Do you think you may have an "anger problem?" Anger is not bad, per se. It's a sign that something is not quite right. Anger is an effect and often has a hidden cause, hurt. You really may have a hurt problem. As with the Ying Yang, the two go hand in hand. Anger is the masculine principle and hurt, the feminine principle.

On a Dr. Phil show, there was an example of a hurt beneath the anger. A woman was concerned that her husband became overly angry when he was watching football games on TV. After examining his background, Dr.

Phil found when the man was a teenager, he had accidentally run over and killed his pre-school sister. This remembrance was somehow activated while he watched sports on TV and had little to do with football games. Once this was discovered and the true hurt pain handled, he no longer was angry during football games. This example shows why it is critical to search for the true cause of the obvious effect, and not just try to change the effect alone. (To change the effect alone, might be to watch less football games on TV.)

As a person who primarily feels hurt rather than anger, I have had to search for the anger beneath it. When I have found both, the issue is easier to resolve because it has become whole. It's the Yin Yang of balance at work again.

Often people say, "I just don't understand why she (he) did that." This person is judging the other as deficient in some way. In reality, they are revealing their own lack of consciousness, judging themselves for not understanding human nature, the cause that produced the effect.

If there is always a cause that comes before an effect, does that mean there are no such things as "miracles?" Does this mean that nothing just happens by magic? Possibly. As St. Augustine said, "Miracles happen, not in opposition to Nature, but in opposition to what we know of Nature."

The universe is orderly because it is always in a cause and effect relationship. Miracles are instances where we haven't discovered the cause. Many inventions we have today would have seemed like something from outer space at the turn of the century — miracles. Explain faxes and computers to someone who was just experiencing the Model T Ford. I remember a computer friend saying to me, in the mid-'60s, that someday people will have computers in their homes. That seemed amazing since at that time whole buildings were needed to house the workings of just one computer.

Might you consider a miracle if a plane flew without a drop of fuel? One took off from Payerne, Switzerland, April 2010, on an around-the-world flight. Its name, Solar Impulse, gave the clue — it was solar-powered. However, it moves too slow for commercial use today.

There is yet a higher level of awareness beyond the linear thinking of basic cause and effect, something coming before and something coming after. The beginning cause is really the result of an effect before it. The end effect is the cause of what comes next. One would not be able to label any part as only a cause or an effect. There is no beginning and no end. Perhaps the helix again is a good symbol, mixing and intertwining and expanding. Like with the previous chapter, all this usually happens in the unseen, so we are not aware of it.

How do you see cause and effect occurring together in your life?

_____

_____

_____

_____

_____

_____

Principle #5: Change is a Constant

How do you feel about change? Excited? Fearful? Change is, and can be your friend or foe. Heraclitus (540 BC to 480 BC) said, "Nothing endures but change." If you have a fearful nature, you may feel threatened that things will get worse. If you have a hopeful nature, you may feel encouraged things will get better.

What's the change about? Some changes can be more threatening than others. Does the change involve something that feels far removed, like an event in a different state or a foreign country? Or does the change have to do with you personally and your close relationships. Will there be a surprise test in math today? Will your best friend still like you? Will your parents get a divorce? Has someone you've been with come down with COVID-19?

Often we resist change, no matter what kind. "The beast we know is better than the beast we don't know." How different life would be if we didn't resist change. We'd have less stress, for sure.

The world does not revolve around us, although we expect stability. We need to be gentle with ourselves regarding change, to lessen the stress we feel. Change is about timing. We don't know enough and see enough yet. It is Divine Timing, and only the Divine (The All/our Higher Self/God) understands it.

Everything is changing. Everything is evolving for increased adaptability and interrelationship. The Exploratorium in San Francisco, California once had a demonstration called the "Living Beating Cells Floor Exhibit."

It shows that heart cells beat independently, but, when two cells are placed next to each other, they coordinate to beat together, communicating with each other.

Understanding interrelationship is in our best interest because all things are designed to work together, which is to be in the flow with the universal principles. Inwardly, it makes us feel good, safe, understood — and loved.

Since 2016, there have been massive changes in our political systems. Even though the changes have thrown our country into chaos, it could be called Divine Chaos. It's Divine because there is potential for great growth, creativity, and vision. It's Divine because our planet is uncovering the corruption, greed, and hate that was always there. It has to be uncovered before we can move to integrity and responsibility. The change is positive, although it may not seem so. Remember, chaos is what we call it when we can't see far enough. When the chaos seems too much, too unsettling, we can remember the calming quote, "This too shall pass."

What about looking for ETs? There is an interest in looking for signs of life elsewhere in the universe. In California, the *SETI Institute* and University of California at Berkeley's Radio Astronomy Laboratory have set up a joint project. "Telescopes in Hat Creek are designed to systematically scan the skies for radio signals sent by advanced civilizations from distant star systems and planets." Kryon of Magnetic Service shares that if there are beings out there they don't dare show up. They consider us a too violent society.

Many profound changes we'll be facing in the next few years will be physical and psychological. The geological facts of climate change and possible consequences might produce fear in you for your future. The psychological and spiritual changes that are also occurring can enable you to live without fear, think clearly and maintain an inner peace no matter what occurs.

Are you prepared for change, physically and psychologically? Be flexible and consider it an ally because — change is a constant.

Can you think about something you fear right now, make a change and see the positive side of it? (It's the Yin Yang at work.)

_____

_____

_____

_____

_____

_____

_____

_____

_____

_____

Principle #6: We are Spiritual Beings

You may have heard people talk about spirituality, but are a bit unsure about what that means. The dictionary defines it as "concerning itself with matters of the spirit, regarding humankind's ultimate nature and meaning." These include concepts such as: Who am I? What is life really about? What gives life meaning? These are questions around which our deepest longings and desires are centered.

Most people talk about spirituality in intellectual terms, similar to that above. Recently, I shared with someone what I liked most about spirituality was how practical it is. The person looked at me with a puzzled look. Often people talk about spirituality in vague terms. When I was first learning about spirituality, I was puzzled, too, and the book *There is a Spiritual Solution to Every Problem* by Dr. Wayne Dyer caught my attention. How could spiritually be practical? It's so otherworldly. Isn't it?

Neale Donald Walsch explains the relevance of spirituality:

> The problem facing the world today is spiritual. Your ideas about spirituality are killing you. You keep trying to solve the world's problem as if it was a political problem, or an economic problem, or even a military problem, and it is none of these. It is a spiritual problem. And that is the one problem human beings don't seem to know how to solve.

Perhaps we don't know how to solve it, because we don't understand spirituality. Spirituality holds the key to resolving the negative emotions we encounter every day, such as blame, guilt, worry, depression, and fear, which cause the chaos we see in the world.

Most people equate spirituality with religion, but they are not the same. Religions provide answers to the "who, what, and why" questions, and require that you believe their interpretation. Each religion has its own set of directions and tells us what God is and what He wants of us. Spiritualism does not have rules and regulations, and does not require us to believe anything, but asks us to be aware of our own experience and to resolve the negativities that keep us from understanding and compassion for all people. We are our own authority. We are not to be guided by what others tells us from their experiences. Religion is an institution, and spiritualism is an experience.

Many religions focus on their own prophets instead of God. They look at the tree and marvel, often worship the tree, because of the way it moves in the wind. They don't realize the tree is not moving by itself. The tree is still without the catalyst of the wind. The wind is the power, not the tree. God is the power, not the prophet. The prophet has enabled God to work through him or her.

Not long ago, a friend asked me to define spiritual? I said everything is spiritual because spirituality is an attitude about life. Everything matters and the least little thing may be important. What defines something is the feeling you bring to it. Depending on the person, life can be meaningful and spiritual, or meaningless.

Spiritualism leads us to understand that God is indescribable. If anyone tells you they know what God is, they don't, for God is beyond our knowledge and words. God is in the physical and the spaces that exist in the physical. We've something in common with a chair because God is in us, and in the chair, alike. This is a reason spiritual masters have great respect for everything. Everything and everyone is a part of God.

Spiritualists know that higher consciousness is relayed in a disguised form, so only those who are ready to benefit will understand. They learn about God from everywhere and everything. God talks to us in many ways, and you have to be alert for the unseen. Also, spiritualists know attitudes and feelings are spiritual issues. It's more than what you do, but why you do it, and how you feel about it. Spiritual attitudes are a function of the right side of our brain that handles feelings. In the sitcom, *The Good Place,* people think they are in heaven because of the good deeds they accomplished on earth. As things don't seem to work out as they wished, they realize they are really in hell, because they did their good deeds for the wrong reasons (self-importance and financial gain).

Spiritualists have a conception of forgiveness that is evolving. The need to forgive means someone did something to you that was "bad." You feel you were a victim. You were right and they were wrong, and you blame them for it. Psychologists agree this harms you more than the other. You are reacting to something, so it's a key for you that you have a problem. There is something to investigate for you to become free of it. Why did it bother you so much? Your higher self cannot be harmed, only your ego. And, what would a loving response be instead? What if you viewed the incident as a learning to help you become free. I know this concept is different, but try it the next time you feel wronged.

If you do, you may find it will lift your spirits and you may eventually see you will never need to forgive anyone for anything again because nothing "bad" happened to you.

We are all on a spiritual path whether we are aware of it or not. That is why we came to Earth, to learn (actually remember) who we really are (spiritual beings), and to learn how to resolve the negativity we experience, and transform it into the various expressions of love. We get sidetracked however, and instead think the car, the job, the "soul mate," the house, will fill that deeper need.

Anyone advanced on the true spiritual path is caught up less with the outer, and is most interested in developing a nature that is positive, thankful, peaceful, and devoid of negativity in any form — judgment, hate, blame, fear, non-forgiveness, worry, unrest. That state is held regardless of what is happening to the person or in the world. Our thoughts, attitudes, and actions are the evidence of our spirituality, not by what religion we belong to or profess to believe. The Masters experienced this positive state in totality. For others, traveling a spiritual path is a real workout. We have to catch ourselves in the negativity and change it right away. It is a discipline, as if we were Olympic athletes training for a physical sport. Life gives us example after example to resolve.

It's folly to compare your self with another. You want to discover and advance on your own path. To compare and experience jealousy of another person's path is a detour from your own highest destiny. It would be like changing trains without knowing the destination of the other train and the baggage it carries.

We may or may not realize we are spiritual beings and on a spiritual path in this lifetime. However, we are perfect, following our own path and doing exactly what we came here to do. Again, it's Divine Chaos. We may consider our situation "chaos," while our higher self considers it "divine." Our birthright is to evolve to the highest we can become, to resolve our inner separation and realize our oneness with self, God and all. It is a blessing and hope for us all, and the only hope for the planet.

How do you see spirituality in your life?

_____
_____
_____
_____
_____
_____
_____
_____
_____
_____
_____

Principle #7: It's All About Energy and Vibration

If Pinocchio went to school, he might have been taught about science. In his day and age, however, many scientists were only dreaming of what we know today with quantum physics (the studies of the tiniest parts).

<u>Energy</u>

Basic science teaches us our physical world is made up of matter and energy. It's easier to understand matter because we can see it. Energy is a part of the unseen and more elusive. However, even with a basic understanding of science, we know that matter and energy cannot be created or destroyed. They just change form. The water cycles and plant cycles are physical examples of this.

Are humans any different? Yes and no. Our physical world is a closed system, meaning those elements recycle on earth and its atmosphere. But we are an open system and more than physical, which means we can exchange our energy beyond the earth itself. It has been scientifically proven that we weight less after death than before death? What left us and where did it go? This is the area where science intersects with spirituality.

We are divine, dynamic beings. We recycle too. Our bodies may return to the earth in the closed system, but our souls advance through many lifetimes in the open system. TJ Woodward says, "It's like we are a book, with many chapters." This recycling is called "reincarnation."

The recycling of one's energy is held to be true by most ancient philosophies.

A large proportion of human suffering occurs because people think they only live once. When they become fully aware that the present life is only one point in the eternal flow of time, and that they have lived in the past and will live again in the future, they will understand that their future lives will depend on their present life and also that they can choose what kind of life they will live in the future ...

From the book: *The Essence of Buddha*

Can reincarnation be proven? Yes and No. Not by a double blind study. However, our inklings (thank you, Jiminy) have given us some hints that it may be true. Called "déjà vue," this is when you have felt you have been somewhere or done something before. This is another example where the past, present, and future are one as mentioned in "Time and Space are one" from Chapter 10. You are accessing passed memories. Every cell in our bodies has a memory, called "cell memory." Perhaps that is why child prodigies have amazing talents at very young ages. They are accessing the memories of the past, stored in their cells. You may have already had these sensations of déjà vue and cell memory.

When I was young, I had nightmares about earthquakes and volcanoes. In our 30s, my husband and I were in Herculaneum, Italy, and visited the ruins caused by the earthquakes and eruption of Mt. Vesuvius in 74 AD. We were not able to spend much time there, because I was too upset being in the ruins. Did I die there in one of my past lives?

I feel I may have been one of those cliff divers in Mexico, who dive off cliffs into the ocean. Whenever I get to a high elevation and look down, like off a balcony, or I look down a waterfall, I get the sensation that I want to jump. In my teens, I went with a group of friends to a public pool in San Mateo, California, which had a high dive platform. Everyone was going up and jumping into the pool. I followed, like a lemming. I had no diving experience, but I remembered my mom talking about a swan dive. I executed one perfectly. Smart? No. What was I thinking? Were my cells confident, if not my mind? When I was on a Mediterranean cruise with a girlfriend, I asked her not to let me go alone to the back of the ship where the waters were churning. I was concerned I might jump.

Vibration

Energy vibrates at different levels, or frequencies. The lowest vibrations are those of inanimate objects, like buildings, cars, and furniture. Higher levels are living things like plants, and then animals. From lower to higher, levels go from minerals, to vegetables, to animals. Of the animals, humans have the highest level on earth.

People vibrate at different levels also, depending on their level of consciousness, their thoughts, and their emotions. As far back as the Middle Ages, sensitive and psychic people were able to see energy fields of subtle colors surrounding people and plants. These were called auras and the colors indicated the height of their vibration. Nikola Tesla, in 1891, was the first to take a photograph of an aura. In the 1960s, the Soviet Union did aura research. From 1975, people's auras were photographed worldwide.

Our thoughts occur at different vibrations. The lowest occur when we concern ourselves with people — what they do, what they have, who they are. Middle vibrations are those about current events — politics, economics, our daily schedules. The highest vibrations are those of universal principles and values.

Peace and happiness are high vibrations. We are like radios and can only receive these vibrations if we have the instrument to do so. How do we develop our instrument to receive these higher levels?

1) Being guided by one's higher self more than one's ego

2) Having little reaction if someone pushes one of your buttons

3) Being more outer-focused than self-focused

4) Seeing change as a friend and being able to flow with life

5) Asking how can I give instead of what's in it for me

6) Knowing that everything that happens will include a learning

7) Having no one left to forgive

8) Seeing the oneness of all without any separation, especially between people

If you don't believe in reincarnation, "entertain" the thought. It's okay to be skeptical. It's a new thought to many.

What do you think about the concept of reincarnation?

___

Have you experienced déjà vue in your life? What conclusions did you draw from it?

___

In what vibrational level do you think you operate most of the time? (1 = negative, in deep despair, 5=midpoint, 10 = enlightened, a mystic and sage.[1])

_____

_____

_____

_____

_____

_____

_____

_____

* * * * * *

Time to celebrate! Just by reading *The Universal Principles Book for Life*, you have earned the equivalent of a college undergraduate degree in life, understanding how to become free.

Note: Many of the concepts in this chapter may also be found in McCulley's first book, *Finding the Lost UNIVERSAL PRINCIPLES. The Three Little Pigs unlock the door.* Interdimensional Press, 2010

[1] *Power vs. Force* by Dr. David Hawkins has a chart showing the vibrational levels of humans that might be helpful.

NOTES

THE DEFINITION OF SUCCESS

To Pinocchio, success first meant freedom from not having Geppetto pull his strings anymore, freedom to go where he wanted, and do what he wanted. As he experienced life, he found to be a "real boy" he needed to be "brave, truthful and unselfish." He was successful because he learned from his experiences. He was able to overcome his lying, his laziness, his lack of judgment and his self-involvement. At his own risk, he saved his father from the belly of the whale.

Our current culture does not define success as being "brave, truthful and unselfish." What a different world we would have if that were so. Today, success means having money, or status or power, or all of them. "Whomever has the most toys at death wins." That's studying from the old textbook because outer possessions and titles will not bring ultimate satisfaction. And that is why so many people are so unhappy. Success is being happy and peaceful, getting the right answers to the "How To Be Happy and Peaceful" Test. Congratulations, you have a head start because you now have the book, *The Universal Principles Book for Life*, to study for the test.

Here's the good news and the bad news. That book on principles you just read are for the symbolic levels of learning, which cover middle school, high school and undergraduate studies in college. These were lecture type courses. You have received information on what you can't count on — physical things, wealth, and other people. You have information on what you can count on — oneness, balance, the power of the unseen, the blending of cause and effect, the reality of change, your nature as a spiritual being, the truth about energy and vibration, and how to attain true freedom. Congratulations on your degrees.

But wait, it's not over. Schooling is life-long. "Never stop learning, because life never stops teaching."
—Unknown

Do you want to go on to a higher degree? You don't have to decide right away, but maybe you've already made up your mind because perhaps you've audited some of the courses already.

With the Master's degree, there will not only be other textbooks[1], but also lab courses also involving practice. Mastery will be emphasized in not only intellectual learning but also applying the concepts in everyday life.

You're going to apply what you've learned to yourself, the people you meet every day, and difficult situations.

> No amount of reading or memorizing will make you successful in life. It is the understanding and application of wise thought that counts.
> —Bob Proctor

Here, compassion will be forming. You'll begin to see how others are a mirror of yourself. For example, if you judge another person as lazy, you'll see and accept you've got a lazy side, also. Your stories of what your parents and others did to you will pale as you see there's learning from the experiences, and you will begin to feel gratitude for the balance and resolution as with the Yin Yang.

Perhaps you even feel a calling to do a Ph.D., not "piled high and deep" as sometimes it is affectionately called. It's really Plunge Heartily into Depth, uncovering the magnificence of who you really are. Here, *Being* is emphasized. With the Ph.D., there are no lectures, only lab courses[2]. You will discover as you surrender *from* your old stories and strings, you will start to surrender *to* a higher vibration. Rather than just learning about and trying to aspire to love, compassion, forgiveness, and kindness, you'll *Be* loving, compassionate forgiving, and kind. Here, instead of trying to attract a quality as with The Law of Attraction, you will begin to see this is your birthright and will affirm you are that already.

There will be nothing outer to do. It will be inner work. Very few receive this degree and very few even want it, but it is possible. It's always more magnificent than you can imagine. You will be free.

Isn't it time to remember who you were before the world told you who you should be?"
—Anonymous

These degrees are the roadmap for true success in life and will bring you the freedom, happiness, and the peace you desire.

The degrees from middle school, high school, undergraduate college, a Master's and a Ph.D. written here don't mean you are actually at a physical school studying those, not even on the Internet. They are symbolic. It's possible you didn't get your GED from high school, but are practicing at a symbolic Master's level of consciousness.

Then, too, some have always had the wrong textbooks to study for true success even though they gained an actual Ph.D. from a university.

What does success mean to you?

_____
_____
_____
_____
_____
_____
_____
_____
_____
_____
_____
_____
_____
_____

Which degree (high school, Master's, Ph.D.) appeals to you and why?

_____

_____

_____

_____

_____

_____

_____

_____

_____

Blessings on your choices as you travel the road of life.

---

[1] The book, *Letting Go . . . The Pathway to Surrender*, by Dr. David Hawkins, mentioned in the previous chapter, is helpful for receiving your Master's.

[2] One required lab course would be on meditation. "It is only through retreat rather than pursuit, through inaction rather than action, that we acquire wisdom." —Lao Tzu

NOTES

FINAL THOUGHTS
YOU'RE THE ONE WE'VE BEEN WAITING FOR

Pinocchio applauds you. You are so much more than he could have ever dreamed for himself. Do you realize how magnificent you are right now as a human being? You are a dynamic, spiritual being and a success story.

Physicists tell us we're actually made of stardust. Nearly all the elements in the human body were made in a star and many have come through several supernovas. Happenings had to be synchronized for 13 to 14 billion years for you to be born. Stop for a moment and take that in.

Scientists state both fossil and genetic evidence indicate Neanderthals and modern humans (Homo sapiens) evolved from a common ancestor between 500,000 and 200,000 years ago. Your ancestors had to learn to survive, find food, shelter, and protection from those saber-toothed tigers and each other. Some believe portions of the earth were directly populated by star beings, the Pleiadians and the Sirians, to name two.

Whatever the source, happenings had to be in perfect synchronicity for billions of years for you to be here today. Think for a moment about all the right moments that had to happen in the cosmos and with all of your ancestors to meet in the right timing, circumstance, their biological clocks aligned physically and emotionally. All those things had to go right, within seconds. So now, it's all come down to you. Why do you think you were born?

Are you aware of your purpose?

_____
_____
_____
_____
_____
_____

Are you aware of your destiny?

_____
_____
_____
_____
_____
_____

You may only have an inkling. Most people spend their entire lives trying to discover their purpose. After all, it's the Ph.D. of consciousness, because in addition to an outer purpose there is an inner purpose. You discover your outer purpose (what job or profession you will *Have*), but you uncover your inner purpose (how you will *Be*). To uncover your inner purpose, you clear the negativities you have built up over the years. Weed your garden. Purposes may change and expand as you experience life and lessons.

We elders hope you will stand on our shoulders and advance the consciousness of the planet, not just study and talk about joy, love, kindness, wonder, and compassion, but *Be* them. *Be free*. The advancement happens every day in every moment. Each moment is new. One doesn't have to be moneyed or hold a position of power. You are perfect just as you are, a divine dynamic being.

You were not an accident. In reading this book, you have shown that this is not your first time here. You chose to be here for a purpose to contribute to humanity in some way. It is your challenge to discover what gift is yours to bring.

Thank you for being.
You're the one we've been waiting for.

Written with love,

Patricia McCulley
Brentwood, California
2020
(The year of clear sight amidst the duality in the world.)

Acknowledgments

I forever thank Creative Initiative Foundation for helping me understand and apply the Universal Principles, which I detail in *Breaking Strings*. I started to become aware of them in my 30s, and since then they have been solid ground on which I've built my life. At first, I had one or two principles, but then added insights from my spiritual and psychological teachers, Sylvia Browne, Kryon of Magnetic Service channeled by Lee Carroll, Neale Donald Walsch, TJ Woodward, Dr. Joe Dispenza, Paul Selig, Michael J. Allen, Father Tom Bonacci, and Matthew Fox.

Special thanks to SJ Farry, for writing a special chapter on school, and offering feedback on my manuscript from a 19 year-old's perspective. I just wish we had had more time together before you scooted off to Brigham Young University.

I could not have done this book without help from my husband, Byron, who is the formatting extraordinaire. He helped design the front and back covers, and added illustrations to the book where needed. He also had to put up with my odd sleeping patterns, since many times I was up at 3:00 am or 4:00 am with an inspiration, then couldn't get back to sleep, which led to challenging days.

Sue Clark, my editor, has been a help to me for over 10 years, starting with my first book. You are valued as an editor, an advisor, and a friend.

Thank you my friend of over 30 years, Susan ten Bosch Paull, for her detailed work with the manuscript and general sounding board. Thanks also to her husband, Arthur Paull, psychotherapist, who contributed to the chapter on sexuality from his perspective of working with young people who suffered from abuse.

Thank you Daphne Saurman, my granddaughter, who reviewed some of my chapters with me. You are loved and appreciated. Comments from my son, Matthew McCulley, were appreciated and valued highly.

Others who have given me suggestions for the book were Rev. Robert Walden, Ruthanne Kohutek, Steve Shearer, Don Huntington and Ron Viera.

I thank all of the experiences in my life. Every one I have been able to resolve and learn from. As an elder, it is my time to share what I have learned about freedom, for I am free.

Appendix A

WHALE IN JAIL

A few years ago, a female humpback whale had become entangled in a spider web of crab traps and lines.

She was weighted down by hundreds of pounds of traps that caused her to struggle to stay afloat. She also had hundreds of yards of line rope wrapped around her body, her tail, her torso, and a line tugging in her mouth.

A fisherman spotted her just east of the Farallon Islands (outside the Golden Gate) and radioed for help.

Within a few hours, the rescue team arrived and determined that she was so bad off, the only way to save her was to dive in and untangle her; a very dangerous proposition. One slap of the tail could kill a rescuer.

They worked for hours with curved knives, and eventually freed her.

When she was free, the divers say she swam in what seemed like joyous circles. She then came back to each and every diver, one at a time, nudged them, and pushed gently, thanking them. Some said it was the most incredibly beautiful experience of their lives.

The guy who cut the rope out of her mouth says her eye was following him the whole time, and he will never be the same.

May you, and all those you love, be so fortunate — to be surrounded by people who will help you get untangled from the things that are binding you.

And, may you always know the joy of giving and receiving gratitude.[1]

Note from the author: Other people may help you become untangled. But be sure to listen to your higher self, Jiminy.

---

[1] SFGATE, Wednesday, December 14, 2005. "Daring rescue of whale off Farallones / Humpback nuzzled her saviors in thanks after they untangled her from crab lines, diver says."
https://www.sfgate.com/bayarea/article/Daring-rescue-of-whale-off-Farallones-Humpback-2557146.php#photo-2699481

Appendix B

THIS SHOULD BE POSTED IN ALL SCHOOLS AND WORK PLACES

Love him or hate him, he sure hits the nail on the head with this! Bill Gates recently gave a speech at a High School about 11 things they did not and will not learn in school. He talks about how feel - good, politically correct teachings created a generation of kids with no concept of reality and how this concept set them up for failure in the real world.

Rule 1: Life is not fair – get used to it!

Rule 2: The world won't care about your self-esteem. The world will expect you to accomplish something BEFORE you feel good about yourself.

Rule 3: You will NOT make $60,000 a year right out of high school. You won't be a vice-president with a car phone until you earn both.

Rule 4: If you think your teacher is tough, wait till you get a boss.

Rule 5: Flipping burgers is not beneath your dignity. Your Grandparents had a different word for burger flipping: they called it opportunity.

Rule 6: If you mess up, it's not your parents fault, so don't whine about your mistakes, learn from them.

Rule 7: Before you were born, your parents weren't as boring as they are now. They got that way from paying your bills, cleaning your clothes and listening to you talk about how cool you thought you were. So before you save the rain forest from the parasites of your parent's generation, try delousing the closet in your own room

Rule 8: Your school may have done away with winners and losers. But life HAS NOT. In some schools, they have abolished failing grades and they'll give you as MANY TIMES as you want to get the right answer. This doesn't bear the slightest resemblance to ANYTHING in real life.

Rule 9: Life is not divided into semesters. You don't get summers off and very few employers are interested in helping you FIND YOURSELF. Do that on your own time.

Rule 10: Television is NOT real life. In real life people actually have to leave the coffee shop and go to jobs.

Rule 11: Be nice to nerds. Chances are you'll end up working for one.

IF YOU AGREE PASS THIS ON IF YOU CAN READ IT THANK A TEACHER

Appendix C

Rules For Being Human

(from an old Ann Landers syndicated newspaper column)

<u>You will receive a body</u>. You may like it or hate it, but it will be yours for as long as you live. How you take care of it or fail to take care of it can make an enormous difference in the quality of your life.

<u>You will learn lessons</u>. You are enrolled in a full-time school called Life. Each day, you will be presented with opportunities to learn what you need to know. The lessons presented are often completely different from those you THINK you need.

<u>There are no mistakes—only lessons</u>. Growth is a process of trial and error and experimentation. You can learn as much from failure as you can from success.

<u>A lesson is repeated until it is learned</u>. A lesson will be presented to you in various forms until you have learned it. When you have learned it (as evidenced by a change in your attitude and behavior), then you can go on to the next lesson.

<u>"There" is no better than "here."</u> When your "there" has become a "here," don't be fooled by believing that the unattainable is better than what you have.

<u>Others are merely mirrors of you.</u> You cannot love or hate something about another person unless it reflects something you love or hate about yourself. When tempted to criticize others, ask yourself why you feel so strongly.

<u>What you make of your life is up to you</u>. You have all the tools and resources you need. Remember that through desire, goal-setting and unflagging effort, you can have anything you want.

<u>Persistence is the key to success.</u> The answers lie within you. The solutions to all of life's problems lie within your grasp. All you need to do is ask, look, listen and trust.

<u>You will forget all this</u>. Unless you consistently stay focused on the goals you have set for yourself, everything you've just read won't mean a thing.

Appendix D

The Four Agreements

1. Make No Assumptions.

2. Keep Your Agreements.

3. Take Nothing Personally.

4. Always Give Your Best.

—Don Miguel Ruiz

Appendix E

Do not believe in anything simply because you have heard it.

Do not believe in anything simply because it is spoken and rumored by many.

Do not believe in anything simply because it is found written in your religious books.

Do not believe in anything merely on the authority of your teachers and elders.

Do not believe in traditions because they have been handed down for many generations.

But after observation and analysis, when you find that anything agrees with reason and is conducive to the good and benefit of one and all, then accept it and live up to it.

Addendum: Listen to your heart.

—Gautama Buddha

Also by Patricia Pillard McCulley

Finding the Lost UNIVERSAL PRINCIPLES
The Three Little Pigs unlock the door.

My Unexpected Christmas Gift

www.ingramcontent.com/pod-product-compliance
Lightning Source LLC
LaVergne TN
LVHW091550060526
838200LV00036B/773